Border Ireland

When the 1998 Good Friday Agreement brought an end to decades of conflict, which was mainly focused on the existence of the Irish border, most breathed a sigh of relief. Then came Brexit. *Border Ireland: From Partition to Brexit* introduces readers to the Irish border. It considers the process of bordering after the partition of Ireland to the Good Friday Agreement and attendant debordering to the post-Brexit landscape. The UK's departure from the EU meant rebordering in some form. That departure also reinvigorated the push for a 'united Ireland' and borderlessness on the island.

As well as providing a nuanced assessment that will be of interest to followers of UK/Irish relations and European studies, this book's analysis of processes of bordering/debordering/rebordering helps inform our understanding of borders more generally. Students and scholars of European studies, border studies, politics, and international relations, as well as anyone else with a general interest in the Irish border will find this book an insightful and historically grounded aid to contemporary events.

Cathal McCall is Professor of European Politics and Borders at Queen's University, Belfast, UK.

Routledge Borderlands Studies

Borderlands are spaces of transition between cultures, societies and states. Often, like in the case of the US and Mexico, they are understood as static territorial lines and buffer zones, subservient to the development of states and state territories. However, borderlands can also be fluid and ambiguous spaces, moulded by processes of economic and political integration or shifting geopolitical dividing lines. Moreover, borderlands cultures can be found far from borders, in cities, multicultural neighbourhoods and diasporic communities. They also exist as both future-oriented geographical imaginations and imaginaries with profound historical roots. Today, globalisation, integration and new transnational forms of communication change the complex interrelationships between state, society, space and borders. Consequently, borderlands become more and more places in their own right, reflecting broader supranational patterns of political, economic and social change.

With this series we encourage inter- and multidisciplinary investigation on borders and borderlands throughout the world. We engage with the political, social and historical richness of borderlands, reflecting their unique (geo) political and cultural significance in contexts of colonial rule, nation-building and integration. The Series will explore, among other things, shifting social and political relations and place-related identities that emerge in borderlands, as well as cross-border interaction and the historical memories of every-day life at borders. With this series, we will both contribute to the rich tradition of North American and European borderlands studies and provide a forum for new growing interest in research on borderlands in Africa, Asia and Latin America.

Remapping Security on Europe's Northern Borders
Edited by Jussi P. Laine, Ilkka Liikanen and James W. Scott

Border Ireland
From Partition to Brexit
Cathal McCall

For more information about this series, please visit: www.routledge.com/Routledge-Borderlands-Studies/book-series/BORDERLAND

Border Ireland

From Partition to Brexit

Cathal McCall

Routledge
Taylor & Francis Group
LONDON AND NEW YORK

First published 2021
by Routledge
2 Park Square, Milton Park, Abingdon, Oxon OX14 4RN

and by Routledge
605 Third Avenue, New York, NY 10158

Routledge is an imprint of the Taylor & Francis Group, an informa business

British Library Cataloguing-in-Publication Data
A catalogue record for this book is available from the British Library

Library of Congress Cataloging-in-Publication Data
Names: McCall, Cathal, 1966- author.
Title: Border Ireland: from partition to Brexit/Cathal McCall.
Description: Abingdon, Oxon; New York, NY: Routledge, 2021. | Series: Routledge borderlands studies | Includes bibliographical references and index.
Identifiers: LCCN 2021005895 (print) | LCCN 2021005896 (ebook) | ISBN 9781138587045 (hardback) | ISBN 9781032047997 (paperback) | ISBN 9780429504211 (ebook)
Subjects: LCSH: European Union—Ireland. | European Union—Great Britain. | Ireland—Boundaries—Northern Ireland. | Northern Ireland—Boundaries—Ireland. | Ireland—History—Partition, 1921.
Classification: LCC HC240.25.I73 M23 2021 (print) | LCC HC240.25.I73 (ebook) | DDC 341.242/209415—dc23
LC record available at https://lccn.loc.gov/2021005895
LC ebook record available at https://lccn.loc.gov/2021005896

ISBN: 978-1-138-58704-5 (hbk)
ISBN: 978-1-032-04799-7 (pbk)
ISBN: 978-0-429-50421-1 (ebk)

Typeset in Times New Roman
by Apex CoVantage, LLC

For Charlie and Josie

Contents

Acknowledgements

At the Queen's University of Belfast, I have been fortunate to enjoy the comradeship of my long-standing border studies compadres James Anderson, Hastings Donnan, Liam O'Dowd, and Tom Wilson. I have also reaped the rewards of collegiality in the School of History, Anthropology, Philosophy, and Politics and across the university, with special gratitude to Elizabeth Meehan and to Aine Egan, Valerie Miller, Emma Derleta, Viviane Gravey, Debbie Lisle, David Phinnemore, Lee McGowan, Timofey Agarin, Peter McLoughlin, Yvonne Galligan, Richard English, Margaret O'Callaghan, Brendan O'Leary, John Coakley, Keith Breen, Margaret Topping, Caroline McNeill, Cillian McBride, Scott Dixon, Elodie Fabre, John Garry, Mark Phelan, Dave Robb, Des O'Rawe, John Morison, Brian Mercer Walker, Maria Adriana Deiana, and Milena Komorova. Special thanks to my PhD student, Darren Litter, who read and commented on a draft of this book.

In 2017–8, I was honoured to be a visiting fellow in the Robert Schuman Centre for Advanced Studies of the European University Institute. Particular thanks to Brigid Laffan, Director of Centre. Bons baisers eta besarkadak to Xabier Itçaina, CNRS, Sciences Po Bordeaux, my long-time research colleague and friend. Metaphorical handshakes (we may never again know the real thing) to James Scott, Ilkka Liikanen, and Jussi Laine, University of Eastern Finland, for rewarding research collaboration on EUBORDERSCAPES. Thanks also to my former PhD student Amalia Campos Delgado, Leiden University, for a delightful supervision experience and enlightening discussions on Mexico as a border zone.

Another former PhD student (and now a co-author), Jaume Castan Pinos, University of Southern Denmark (USD), continues to be tirelessly inquisitive and an ongoing torture, happily endured, long after he flew the supervisory coop. I am also grateful to his colleagues at USD, Katarzyna Stokłosa, Dorte Jagetic Andersen, Steen Bo Frandsen, and Martin Klatt, for fruitful academic engagement on borders and border regions research. As always, sincere thanks to James Mitchell, University of Edinburgh, and to the staff at the National Library of Scotland.

To my sisters, Anne and Marie, their unending love and support are a bedrock. My deepest debt of gratitude is to my darling wife, Erin, and our beloved girls, Marielle and Méabh. Much of this book was written during 2020 when a wretched pandemic meant working at/from home. It was a pleasure for me to do so, but for them, maybe not so much.

The book is dedicated to my departed mother and father.

Introduction

The Irish border has endured for a century. As such, it is an old European border.[1] The partition that created the border on the island of Ireland emerged from the Government of Ireland Act (1920) and the Anglo-Irish Treaty (1921) which the British government agreed in London with a representation of Irish rebel leaders. The precise contour of the border – along county boundaries dividing 26 counties in 'the South' and 6 counties in 'the North' – was confirmed by British, Irish, and Northern Ireland governments after the Boundary Commission's 1925 report was suppressed.

Over the course of the century, the Irish border experienced processes of bordering and debordering. Bordering began in the 1920s with the construction of border infrastructure and the mobilisation of customs officials and border security personnel. Bordering was advanced by state-building on either side of the border and mutual hostility between government administrations, North and South. That hostility was reflected and enhanced in the print media. Bordering intensified further during the 1970s and 1980s through British security infrastructural reinforcement along the border in response to a concerted Irish Republican Army (IRA) insurgency.

Countervailing debordering commenced in the 1990s as an outcome of Europeanisation and the Irish Peace Process. Their milestones were the Single European Act (1986), delivering the European Single Market on 31 December 1992, and the Good Friday Agreement (1998), respectively. Border customs, inspection, and security infrastructure evaporated, and North–South and cross-border cooperation took root.

The prospect of rebordering on the island of Ireland emerged with the 2016 referendum on the withdrawal of the UK from the EU – popularly known as Brexit (from 'Britain's exit') – and the stunning success of the Leave campaign. From an EU perspective, securing its Single Market and Customs Union required border customs and inspection points with 'Third Countries'.[2] For Brexiters, their 'take back control' mantra necessitated the need for secure 'hard' borders for the United Kingdom of Great Britain and Northern Ireland or, at least, Great Britain. In the UK scenario, the implications of rebordering the 'soft' open Irish border were dispiriting, particularly for Irish nationals. The alternative, an 'Irish Sea Border' which would keep Northern Ireland in the EU in all but name while Great Britain left was ominous for the Ulster British community (Anderson, 2018).

The Brexit negotiation lasted for four years: from the referendum of 2016 to the Withdrawal Agreement of 2019 to the EU–UK Trade and Cooperation Agreement of Christmas Eve 2020. The prospect of rebordering the Irish border during that period gave rise to another one: borderlessness on the island of Ireland via 'united Ireland' referenda, North and South, also known as a 'Border Poll'. Accordingly, this book is organised around the themes of bordering, debordering, rebordering, and borderlessness.

The book draws on, and elaborates on, arguments made by the author in published work including 'Reconfiguring the Border', pp. 43–65 in Katy Hayward and Muiris MacCarthaigh (eds.), *Recycling the State: The Politics of Adaptation in Contemporary Ireland*. Dublin: Irish Academic Press, 2007 (on bordering); *The European Union and Peacebuilding: The Cross-Border Dimension* (Chapter 4). Basingstoke: Palgrave Macmillan, 2014 (on debordering); 'Brexit, Bordering and Bodies on the Island of Ireland', pp. 292–305 in *Ethnopolitics*, no. 17, vol. 3, 2018 (on rebordering); and 'The Division of Ireland and its Foes: The Centenary of Resistance to Partition' (with Jaume Castan Pinos), in *Nations and Nationalism*, 2021 forthcoming, (on borderlessness).

Terminology

The Irish border refers to the land border between the states of Ireland and the UK (including Northern Ireland). It has also been referred to as the UK border on the island of Ireland or, more provocatively, as Britain's border in Ireland. The terms *Northern Ireland* (a member of the United Kingdom of Great Britain and Northern Ireland) and *Ireland* (an independent state) are used throughout. However, also used are their shorthand forms: 'the North' (Northern Ireland) and 'the South' (Ireland). The 'Republic of Ireland' (Ireland) is also featured, as is the 'island of Ireland' (Ireland and Northern Ireland). Perhaps more confusingly, the term *Ireland* is used to mean the 'island of Ireland', including in the title of the book. This is in acknowledgement of the fact that 'Ireland' (the island) is a historical entity and, contemporaneously, remains understood by many at home and abroad to mean the island of Ireland.

The 'Ulster British' refers to the ethnic Ulster Protestant community in Northern Ireland with a national allegiance to Britain and a British national identity. For that community, six-county 'Ulster' is Northern Ireland (a member of the United Kingdom of Great Britain and Northern Ireland). For the Irish, Ulster is a historic nine-county province of Ireland that includes the six counties of 'the North' (Northern Ireland) plus three – Cavan, Donegal, and Monaghan – in 'the South' (Whyte, 1990).

Notes

1 Most of Europe's borders have been created or redrawn by wars in the twentieth century (Poggi, 1990; Tilly, 1990).
2 A Third Country is defined as 'a country that is not a member of the European Union as well as a country or territory whose citizens do not enjoy the European Union right to free movement'. See https://ec.europa.eu/home-affairs/what-we-do/networks/european_migration_network/glossary_search/third-country_en (accessed 10/10/2020).

1 Bordering

Introduction

State borders are imagined as 'lines in the sand' that divide economic, political, and social spaces. They involve a bordering process that encapsulates both border territorial demarcation and the subsequent management of the border in the context of border control. The power of the state is revealed in this demarcation and management.

Binary distinctions are justified and embedded by bordering, that is, distinctions between 'self' and 'other', 'us' and 'them', 'friends' and 'enemies', 'here' and 'there', 'home' and 'abroad', 'domestic' and 'foreign', 'threat' and 'security', and 'include' and 'exclude' (Newman, 2006a, 2006b). State borders are parameters of possession, protection, and exclusion in the national imagination. Within these borders, the nation inhabits a territory, strives to preserve it from incursion by unwanted 'outsiders', and sanctifies it as 'ours, not theirs' through its collective memories and commemorations (Berezin, 2003, p. 7). However, for many nations, the state border cuts through the national territory, undermining the national ideal.

The Irish border was delivered by partition which was enacted by the Government of Ireland Act (1920) and confirmed by the Anglo-Irish Treaty (1921). The treaty was agreed between the British government and a delegation of Irish republicans led by Michael Collins, a commander of the Irish Republican Army (IRA) and Dáil Éireann (Irish parliament, TD).[1] Dáil Éireann ratified the Treaty on 7 January 1922 by a slim majority[2] and, therefore, acquiesced to the partition of Ireland. Thus, two separate polities were created on the island: the Irish Free State (which became the Republic of Ireland in 1949)[3] and Northern Ireland which remained a member of the United Kingdom of Great Britain and Northern Ireland.

The Irish border, which separates the two polities, is 499 km long and coincides with county boundaries that were fully established in the early seventeenth century (Rankin, 2005). It is 'the line in the sand' – or, more accurately, the line in the bog, the field, the lough, the town, the townland, and even the house – that divided the island of Ireland economically, politically, and socially.[4] The power of the British state as an empire in retreat ensured its creation (Anderson and O'Dowd, 2007).

Brendan O'Leary defines *partition* as

> a fresh border cut through at least one community's national homeland, creating at least two separate units under different sovereigns or authorities. The usual justification of such a partition is that it will reduce or resolve a national, ethnic, or communal conflict, but its opponents usually protest the freshness, the artificiality of dividing a national homeland, illegitimately 'tearing' it apart.
>
> (2019a, p. 370)

Irish nationalists were the opponents of partition while Ulster British unionists became the justifiers. The border served to embed a binary distinction between Irish nationalist (nominally Catholic) and Ulster British unionist (nominally Protestant) communities and identities and, for Ulster British unionists, to sanctify Northern Ireland as 'ours, not theirs'.[5]

Prior to partition, and certainly before the Home Rule crisis (1910–4), Ulster Protestants generally regarded themselves to be Irish. After all, the whole of Ireland was part of the United Kingdom of Great Britain and Ireland wherein English, Irish, Scottish, and Welsh identities could be conceived of as complementary to an umbrella British identity. However, the rise of Irish republicanism and partition ruptured the link between Britishness and Irishness. Irish unionism retreated into Ulster unionism and became a Protestant British nationalism with its own *de facto* territory of Northern Ireland – 'ours, not theirs' – largely left to its own devices by the British government and able to pursue its exclusionary cultural, economic and political interests, and identity (O'Leary, 2019a, p. 359). Irish nationals in Northern Ireland, accounting for approximately one-third of the population, were marooned in a territory that became 'theirs, not ours'.

After the partition of the island of Ireland became a reality bordering was driven by state-building on both sides of the border and by antagonism between the Irish state and the Ulster British unionist administration in Northern Ireland. However, in the public sector, a significant degree of 'quiet', practical North–South cooperation led by senior civil servants was evident (Kennedy, 2000). Between 1959 and 1965, North–South cooperation became 'loud' and political. It was embodied by the *rapprochement* between Irish Taoiseach (prime minister) Seán Lemass and Northern Ireland prime minister Terence O'Neill. The decades-long violent conflict known as 'the Troubles', beginning in 1969, ended this period of North–South *rapprochement.*

Despite 'the Troubles', bordering remained incomplete. When the balance of violent conflict shifted from urban centres to the Irish border in the 1980s, British security forces had trouble coping with local mobile IRA units whose insurgents had an in-depth knowledge of the complex border terrain. Despite this challenge, the British border security regime remained spatially patchy. The British government recognised that a continuous, 'hard', securitised border would pay political dividends for Irish republican insurgents and would risk further alienating Irish nationalist borderlanders and the wider Irish national population on the island and further afield.

Oppositional antagonism to bordering was periodically evident in the peripheral and marginalised borderlands, where borderlanders were confronted with border infrastructure and closed border roads. Those who engaged in oppositional antagonism, domestic and commercial smuggling, and other acts of evasion from state authority offered some economic and social compensation (Leary, 2016).

This chapter begins with a consideration of the concepts of borders and bordering. It then charts the course of 'line in the sand' bordering on the island of Ireland from 1921 and details opposition to it. It also outlines countervailing North–South cooperation initiatives and the partiality of the border security regime during the Troubles. Finally, it considers the impact of bordering on borderland communities.

Borders and bordering

The raison d'être of state borders is to divide a territory into political, economic, and social spaces. An understanding of borders and bordering is informed by the analytical lens employed. In magisterial overviews of border studies, geographer David Newman navigated different approaches to studying borders and bordering that have been associated with different academic disciplines. Geographers have conceptualised borders as 'lines in the sand' that divide economic, political, and social spaces and are driven by a bordering process entailing both demarcation and management functions. Political scientists have tended to focus on the power relations involved in that demarcation and management (including border reconfiguration). Sociologists and anthropologists have been primarily concerned with binary distinctions when studying borders, that is distinctions between 'self' and 'other', 'us' and 'them', 'friends' and 'enemies', 'here' and 'there', 'home' and 'abroad', 'domestic' and 'foreign', 'threat' and 'security', and 'include' and 'exclude'(Newman, 2006a, pp. 143–7, 2006b, p. 176).[6]

The contemporary thesis that borders and border guards are everywhere and that bordering is an open-ended process involving the profiling and surveillance of whole populations has become increasingly salient as states and blocs of states seek to control migratory flows, that is who shall be included and who shall be excluded. Border technologies are of central interest in this thesis, as are border guards, employers, landlords, educationalists, and other 'gatekeepers' who are co-opted as participants in a border security regime (Amoore, 2006; Sassen, 2014; Topak et al., 2015).

The borders are everywhere thesis is the preserve of 'critical border studies', a sub-discipline of international relations, which concentrates on the borders/security nexus. Herein, borders 'beyond the line in the sand', that is the multifarious nodes of a state security regime, are of central importance (Parker et al., 2009) Amilhat-Szary and Girant attempted to encapsulate this approach in their 'borderities' concept which considers 'the multiple rules and experiences of what a border can be' (2015, p. 30). 'Critical border studies' implies that border studies is uncritical and passé, not least because state territorial borders and border regions are its key point of departure. However, Liam O'Dowd cautioned that

> much contemporary border study lacks an adequate historical analysis of state and nation formation: they over-emphasise the novelty of contemporary forms of border change and globalization and, in the process, fail to register the extent to which we continue to live in a 'world of diverse states', shot through with the legacy of empires, past and present'.
>
> (2010, p. 1034)

From this border studies perspective, the 'line in the sand' remains the central focus for bordering, debordering, and rebordering in twenty-first-century Ireland as it was in the twentieth century.

Challenges to bordering Ireland, 1920–60

Challenges to bordering Ireland were evident from the outset. Initially, the Government of Ireland Act (1920) made provision for a Council of Ireland to act as an institutional bridge between two devolved parliaments in Ireland, one in the North and one in the South. At the second reading of the bill on 29 March 1920, James Macpherson (chief secretary for Ireland) claimed that the Council of Ireland could become 'virtually a Parliament for all Ireland, and from that stage to complete union is but a very slight and very easy transition'.[7] Section 2(1) of the 1920 act outlined the functions of the council as facilitating harmonious action between the two parliaments, the promotion of a common approach to all-island matters, and the administration of services that were amenable to an all-island approach.[8] However, this outline was vague. The lack of specificity combined with the dynamics of divergent Irish nationalist and Ulster British unionist political aspirations, violence, and state-building on both sides of the border conspired to fatally undermine the Council of Ireland (Tannam, 1999).

Ulster British unionists focused on the establishment of a Northern Ireland government and parliament from scratch and had little interest in the Council of Ireland (Buckland, 2001, p. 212). Meanwhile, the Irish Free State government was unenthusiastic about the Council of Ireland because participation would symbolise its recognition of the Northern parliament and a border which excluded the six counties of Northern Ireland from the thirty-two-county Irish national territorial ideal. In the event, divergent nationalist/unionist political aspirations, separate state-building in the Irish Free State and Northern Ireland, and North–South antagonism fuelled the bordering ahead.

The Craig/Collins Pacts of 1922 – made between Michael Collins, then head of the Provisional Government in the South (with Arthur Griffith), and Sir James Craig, the first prime minister of Northern Ireland – offered brief hope for the incremental development of North–South political cooperation between the Irish Free State and Northern Ireland. One of the terms of the first pact that Collins and Craig agreed to was that '[t]he two governments to endeavour to devise a more suitable system than the Council of Ireland for dealing with problems affecting all Ireland'.[9] Their agreement intimated that the new Irish border could be configured as a political, economic, cultural, and intellectual bridge between the two new polities on the island rather than as a barrier between them.

Such a configuration had potential advantages for Ulster British unionists in Northern Ireland. According to historian of Irish unionism Alvin Jackson, 'Irish Toryism supplied much of the organizational infrastructure around which unionism was constructed; and supplied trained advocates to the loyalist cause' (2001, p. 116). To continue to avail of this advocacy would have provided unionism with an important defence against Irish nationalist foes. Moreover, key Irish institutions, including Trinity College Dublin and the island's main newspaper, *The Irish Times*, remained supportive of Irish unionism. Therefore, the intellectual and cultural cornerstones of Irish unionism in the South remained potentially valuable for Ulster British unionism in a project to build an intellectually and culturally robust Northern Ireland. However, the primary objective of Ulster British unionism was to 'keep Ulster [Northern Ireland] Protestant'. That meant that Southern Protestants – 11.68 per cent of the population of southern

Ireland in 1911 – were effectively disbarred from unionism (Ferriter, 2019, pp. 11–12).

Sir James Craig's incentive for North–South cooperation was the possibility of the recognition of Northern Ireland by the Irish Free State government. For Craig, such cooperation would provide the means for securing the principle of consent in North–South relations, that is that the consent of the Ulster British unionist community would be required for 'Ulster' to join an all-Ireland state (Bew, 1999, p. 407).

In turn, the pacts enabled Michael Collins to become the representative of Northern Catholics for whom he had genuine concern (Laffan, 1983, p. 98; Kennedy, 1999, p. 80). However, Collins also continued to pursue a non-recognition policy for Northern Ireland (Bew, 1999, p. 408). Moreover, the IRA, with encouragement from Collins, continued to engage in violence north of the border (Laffan, 1983, pp. 96–7). In an effort to end violence and reform the police in Belfast, the two leaders entered into a second pact. That pact also failed to deliver primarily because of the lack of an investigation into the alleged role of policemen in sectarian murder in Belfast (Farrell, 1983, pp. 114–7; Laffan, 1983, pp. 92–4; Wilson, 2010).

After the ambush and assassination of Michael Collins at Béal na Bláth on 22 August 1922 during the Irish Civil War, continuing upheaval in the South and the inability, or reticence, of the Provisional Government in dealing with the IRA challenge to Northern Ireland served to bolster the bordering resolve of Ulster British unionist leaders. The unionist conceptualisation of the border as a bulwark against the Irish Free State was informed by the unionist perception of hostility and threat emanating from the South.

The Irish Boundary Commission, which was proposed in the Anglo-Irish Treaty (1921), began work in November 1924 to precisely determine the delineation of the Irish border. Chaired by Robert Feetham, a South African judge, the commission conducted informal meetings, as well as official hearings with more than 500 witnesses interviewed. However, its 1925 report, which recommended only minor adjustments, was suppressed in order to neutralise growing unrest after newspaper forecasts of its findings (Laffan, 1983, p. 103). Instead, the existing border was confirmed in the Boundary Agreement (3 December 1925) by the leaders of the Irish Free State, Northern Ireland, and the British government (Laffan, 1983, p. 105; Leary, 2016, pp. 35–39). Northern nationalists' abandonment was palpable when the Dáil passed the Boundary Agreement on 15 December 1925 (Keogh, 2005, p. 8). Margaret O'Callaghan (1999) concluded that the border became 'copperfastened' as a result.

By 1932, partition was firmly embedded institutionally. As far as the public sector was concerned, Dennis Kennedy painted a stark picture of bordering from partition in 1921 through to the establishment of a republic by the Republic of Ireland Act (1949):

> One of the most remarkable features of the history of the island over the past seventy five years has been, at government level, the near totality of partition, the replacement of a long established single administrative system by two separate administrative systems, which managed, or contrived, to keep all contact to a minimum, which built no new structures, however modest, to take care of common interests in practical matters and which for many decades had no dialogue at all at political level.
>
> (1999, p. 73)

For Kennedy (1999), bordering was a process that was embedded by state-building in the Irish Free State and Northern Ireland and animated by North–South, unionist–nationalist antagonism and hostility in the political and print media milieus.

Despite this institutional embedding of partition violent and political opposition to it remained steadfast. The IRA continued to target British interests in Britain and Northern Ireland. Politically, Éamon de Valera's Fianna Fáil party continued to promote an anti-partitionist line. While this has been dismissed as rhetoric for electoral dividends (Kelly, 2013), de Valera inserted anti-partitionism in Bunreacht na hÉireann|Constitution of Ireland, 1937. According to Article 2, Ireland's 'national territory consists of the whole island of Ireland, its islands and the territorial seas'. This anti-partitionist affirmation was, nonetheless, watered down in Article 3 through the acknowledgement that it was not possible to exercise jurisdiction over all the claimed territory 'pending the re-integration of the national territory'.

The South's constitutional claim to the six counties of Northern Ireland asserted in the 1937 Bunreacht na hÉireann|Constitution of Ireland persisted until the 1998 Good Friday Agreement and fed the myth of siege in the Ulster British communal imagination. The 1937 constitution not only asserted the territorial claim; it also recognised the special position of the Catholic Church in the Irish Free State, reinforcing the commitment of Ulster British unionists to bordering.

The South was not the only source of threat for Ulster British unionists. Threat also emanated from *perfide Albion*. The primary example of British government perfidy occurred in 1940 when British prime minister Winston Churchill offered Irish Taoiseach Éamon de Valera Irish unity in return for granting Allied troops permission to use Irish Free State ports. Set against the Ulster British unionist self-image of being loyal to the British Crown and the reaffirmation of Irish nationalist disloyalty to the Crown through rebellion and the declaration of Ireland's neutrality during World War II, the offer to de Valera served to intensify the sense of existential threat for the Ulster British community emanating from not just from Dublin but from London too (McIntosh, 1999, p. 145; Fanning, 2016).

North–South cooperation: 1960–73

Behind the political scenes, a significant degree of 'quiet', practical North–South cooperation was conducted by senior civil servants. It produced a number of infrastructural and administrative developments, including the Erne hydroelectric scheme; the Foyle Fisheries Commission; the joint operation of the Dublin to Belfast railway line through the Great Northern Railway Board; electricity interconnection; agreements on joint tourism promotion, social welfare payments, extradition of criminals for ordinary crimes; and increased levels of North–South trade (Kennedy, 2000, p. 5).

Beyond the public sector, a plethora of North–South and cross-border organisations and enterprises defied partition and bordering. John Whyte (1983) detailed private- and third-sector organisations continuing to function on an all-island basis after partition. They included businesses, trades unions, banks, professional associations, media and arts organisations, churches and church-affiliated groups, youth and sporting groups, cultural and scientific organisations, and charitable and welfare organisations.[10]

While overt cross-border contact at a political level had proved to be impossible for four decades after the Craig/Collins Pacts, some covert political contact did take place. For example, Seán MacBride (Ireland's minister for external affairs) and Northern Ireland prime minister Sir Basil Brooke had two meetings in 1949 (Arthur, 2000, p. 8). Overt political contact and communication resumed eventually with two meetings in the 1960s involving Ireland's Taoiseach Seán Lemass and Northern Ireland prime minister Captain Terence O'Neill.

After becoming Taoiseach in 1958, Seán Lemass made conciliatory overtures to the unionist government in Northern Ireland. In reference to Northern Ireland during a speech in July 1963, Lemass declared that 'the government and parliament there exists with the support of the majority in the six counties area, artificial though that area is. We see it functioning within its powers . . . within an all Ireland constitution, for as long as it is desired by them' (cited in Mulholland, 2000, p. 80). This qualified recognition of Northern Ireland was enough for O'Neill to be positively disposed to Lemass's call for North–South discussions. However, after subsequent anti-partitionist speeches by Lemass in the United States, O'Neill demurred from immediate face-to-face discussions. It wasn't until Brian

Faulkner (then a minister in the Northern Ireland government) offered to meet Jack Lynch (then Faulker's opposite number in the South) that O'Neill met Lemass at Stormont on 17 January 1965, with a return visit to Dublin on 9 February (Mulholland, 2000, p. 82). O'Neill elected not to inform most of his cabinet colleagues about the first meeting. Consequently, the possibility of duplicity arose in the minds of the uninformed. Moreover, Lemass connected economic cooperation with political cooperation and the ending of partition. While O'Neill remained insouciant about such remarks, other Ulster British unionist politicians felt or feigned rage. Eventually, pressure from the fundamentalist Protestant preacher-turned-politician Reverend Ian Paisley and the threat of revolt from within the ruling ranks of the Unionist Party sundered the Lemass/O'Neill *rapprochement*.

The 1966 commemoration of the 1916 Easter Rising and the arrival of the Northern Ireland civil rights movement dampened prospects for North–South cooperation in the political realm (Kennedy, 1999, p. 85). Paisley used his skills as a populist communicator to particular effect when, in reference to O'Neill, he guldered: '[H]e is a bridge builder he tells us. A traitor and a bridge are very much alike for they both go over to the other side' (quoted in Mulholland, 2000, p. 84). In an innocent prelude to the ravages of the Troubles (beginning in 1969), Ulster British unionist hostility to the O'Neill/Lemass *rapprochement* was expressed in the form of Paisley firing snowballs at Lemass's car as he arrived at Stormont – home of the Northern Ireland Parliament – for a meeting with O'Neill in 1965.

As a preacher and effective orator, Paisley had something in common with the US civil rights leader Martin Luther King Jr. Alas, apart from their Christian beliefs, that was all they shared. The Northern Ireland civil rights movement – mirroring the US civil rights movement's demand for equal citizenship – was vehemently opposed by Paisley. That civil rights movement was pivotal in bringing to an end the Ulster British unionist control of Northern Ireland in the late 1960s.

The Northern Ireland civil rights movement parked the issue of partition and concentrated on citizenship as experienced in a part of the UK state. The movement successfully shone a spotlight on the unequal citizenship experienced by Catholics in employment, in the allocation of public housing, and in political (voting) rights in Northern Ireland (Purdie, 1986; Prince, 2007; Farrell, 2018). The era of 'ours, not there's' was effectively ended. For Brendan O'Leary, 'unionists had built a system of ethnic privilege that they could not easily dissolve without causing disarray among their own ranks. O'Neill lacked a strong internal constituency for reforming unionism' (2019b, p. 192).

The Sunningdale Agreement of December 1973 offered renewed hope for debordering. A new all-island Council of Ireland was proposed as a supplement to a Northern Ireland power-sharing system of government – involving Irish nationalist and Ulster British politicians – which had been provided by the Northern Ireland Constitution Act (1973). This Council of Ireland was to be composed of a Council of Ministers with seven members each drawn from the Northern and Southern governments. The council was to be invested with an executive and harmonising function as well as a consultative role. Decisions were to be passed by unanimous vote. A Consultative Assembly, comprising 30 members each from the Northern Ireland Assembly, and Dáil Éireann was proposed to perform advisory and review functions (Hadfield, 1992, p. 8; Hennessey, 1997, p. 221; McCann and McGrattan, 2017).

For the Irish government, the proposed Council of Ireland represented an instrument for debordering and advancement towards the unification of Ireland. However, the proposed North–South institution proved to be unpalatable for a majority of Ulster British unionists. They viewed it much as the Irish government did, although from a diametrically opposite political perspective. For the Ulster British unionists, the Council of Ireland was the embodiment of a renewed threat to the border with the Republic of Ireland and hence a threat to the existence of Northern Ireland and the Ulster British community. The colourful unionist politician and public relations guru John Laird (later the leading Ulster-Scots cultural entrepreneur Lord Laird of Artigarvan) coined the soundbite 'Dublin is just a Sunningdale Away' to hotwire Ulster British fears and insecurity. Subsequently, the Ulster British loyalist-inspired Ulster Workers' Council strike of 1974 not only stifled the creation of the Council of Ireland; the strike also collapsed the entire edifice of the power-sharing government in Northern Ireland after just five months.

The Troubles, beginning in 1969, provided the overriding obstacle to the development of North–South cooperation in the public sphere for two decades to come. Although the main ideological objective of the IRA's campaign of violence was to end partition and destroy the border between North and South, the practical effect of that campaign was to reinforce bordering on the island. Irish republicans (principally the IRA), Ulster British loyalists, and British state security forces fought a protracted 25-year violent conflict primarily over the existence of the border. The IRA was actually fighting two wars simultaneously. One was with the British state security forces. It was anti-partitionist and focused on destroying the border. The other was with Ulster British loyalist paramilitary forces which had an ethnonationalist thrust (Castan Pinos and McCall, 2021).

The Troubles claimed more than 3,600 lives. In brutal statistical terms, that is 0.2 per cent of a population of 1,750,000. In contrast, the conflict in Colombia (1965–2016) resulted in more than 200,000 deaths or 0.04 per cent of a population of 49,400,000. Thus, the Troubles may be interpreted as a relatively intense, long conflict caged mostly within the small territorial confines of Northern Ireland.

Borderland communities

In *Unapproved Routes: Histories of the Irish Border 1922–1972*, Peter Leary vividly depicts the rupture that bordering brought to local borderland communities. He writes of 'the disruption it caused to patterns of everyday life, to concepts of locality based on well-established social, spiritual, and administrative connections, and its impact on long-standing tensions and divisions' (Leary, 2016, p. 56). Such disruption was experienced by the Irish and the Ulster British alike. For example, in Drummully – part of which is in County Monaghan in the South, the rest in County Fermanagh in the North – Protestants residing in the northern part needed to traverse the border to attend church and school or visit the parochial hall and Protestant Union hall all located south of the border (Leary, 2016, p. 39).

Irish border customs checkpoints or 'customs huts' were established in 1923. In 1923, British and Irish customs authorities also agreed on 15 'Approved Frontier Crossing Points' on cross-border roads for the inspection of goods in daytime hours. Many 'unapproved routes' crossing the border remained open to footfall, but travelling on them by automobile was prohibited.[11] Travellers with contraband on unapproved routes risked detection and penalties enforced by customs patrols. Despite the risks, smuggling became a widespread feature of borderland life between the 1920s and the 1960s as borderlanders sought to avoid paying duty on goods bought on the other side of the border.[12]

Invariably, stories of smuggling during this period are of small-time, domestic transgressions: tea leaves and whiskey concealed underneath a petticoat or in a hot-water bottle during wartime (Ferriter, 2019, p. 46) or a turkey underneath a heavy overcoat at Christmas. Even commercial smuggling stories, usually involving the transport of animal livestock in some unusual way, were told to provoke amusement, even admiration, of the smuggler's ingenuity rather than scorn.[13] The Troubles, beginning in 1969, limited smuggling activities because many unapproved routes were closed or destroyed by the British security forces.

Prior to the Troubles many of those cross-border roads had remained open even if most were 'unapproved routes' that, officially, did not permit travel by motor car or the transport of goods. Some were spiked by the Royal Ulster Constabulary during the IRA's ill-fated 1956–62 border campaign, but wholesale closure did not occur until the Troubles took hold in the early 1970s. At that point, a concerted effort was made by the British security forces to render unapproved routes impassable by cratering or bollarding roads and destroying cross-border bridges. The primary aim of this physical bordering was to hinder the cross-border movement of republican insurgents prior to and after an attack.[14]

Unsurprisingly, the destruction of the extensive cross-border road network also had a deleterious impact on the cross-border movement of people. Crossing the border could be done legitimately via the 15 approved routes, but this often involved a circuitous journey and the daunting prospect of being stopped and quizzed by armed British soldiers at border checkpoints. As a result, these checkpoints offered an additional disincentive for cross-border mobility.

The great Irish novelist Eoin McNamee (2019) characterised the Troubles-era Irish borderland as a 'zone of dystopia'. This dystopian border zone was decorated with militarised checkpoints, watchtowers, cameras, concealed listening devices, and the booby-trapped roadside corpses of IRA 'informers'. It was the site of nightmarish acts like the slaughter of 18 British soldiers by the IRA in the Narrow Water ambush of 1979 and the shooting dead by a British soldier of Aidan McAnespie as he crossed the border at Aughnacloy on his way to a Gaelic football match in 1988. It was the scene of cross-border gun battles between the British security forces and the IRA (Mulroe, 2017). This dystopian border zone was a dark landscape where fear, loathing, and trepidation were the order of the day.

Conclusion

Leading borders studies scholar Vladimir Kolossov has argued that borders configured as barriers are 'not only inefficient but objectively harmful to society and the economy' (Kolossov, 2005, p. 619). Between 1921 and 1998, multifarious political initiatives on the island of Ireland aimed at reconfiguring the Irish border from barrier to bridge failed dismally. Ulster British unionist leaders became increasingly committed to bordering and fortifying the border as a barrier between North and South. Constitutional, perfidious, and violent threats emanating from the Irish government, the British government, and the IRA, respectively, were largely responsible for this commitment. The widening cultural chasm between the Irish and the Ulster British also played a significant underlying role.

There were some notable successes in 'quiet' North–South cooperation under the stewardship of civil servants. However, any hint of political or institutionalised North–South cooperation was met with stiff resistance from Ulster British politicians. After the prolonged cold war between the Irish state and Northern Ireland, which lasted from the 1930s to the 1960s and was stimulated, in large part, by de Valera's 1937 Constitution, a political initiative was launched to invigorate North–South cooperation in the

1960s under the auspices of the Lemass/O'Neill *rapprochement*. However, the initiative of Taoiseach Seán Lemass and Northern Ireland prime minister Captain Terence O'Neill also foundered. Rejectionist Ulster British unionist forces mustered successfully to stop the initiative.

In 1974, the attempted resuscitation of the Council of Ireland model, to complement the new unionist–nationalist power-sharing Northern Ireland Executive, intensified the Ulster British unionist/loyalist backlash against power-sharing involving Irish nationalist politicians in Northern Ireland. The backlash, in the form of a general strike, terminated the life of the Executive after five months and ended hopes for a Council of Ireland.

By 1974, the IRA's 'long war' was in full swing. Its primary objective was to destroy the border. However, its cross-border activities resulted in the wholesale destruction of border crossing points by the British security forces and the securitisation of cross-border arterial routes and border hotspots of republican activity, principally South Armagh. It produced the apotheosis of bordering on the island of Ireland during the 1970s and 1980s.

Borderlanders themselves experienced progressive degradation in their cross-border mobility, and in their economic, social, and cultural life from the 1920s to the 1990s. Small-time smuggling offered a form of compensation for some. However, episodic violence and the complex architecture of border security delivered by the Troubles rendered the Irish border region a zone of dystopia. The border became intimately associated with fear, loathing and trepidation during these deeply troubled times.

Notes

1 Teachta Dála (Deputy to the Dáil).
2 Sixty-four TDs voted in favour of the treaty, and 57 TDs voted against it.
3 Ireland, the state, has existed in different forms and under different names. The Irish Free State was changed to 'Éire' (Ireland) in the 1937 Bunreacht na hÉireann|Constitution of Ireland, which also ended dominion status. Éire became a republic in 1949 with the enactment of the Republic of Ireland Act (1949) and the symbolic declaration of a republic on Easter Monday 1949. More recently, the Republic of Ireland has been referred to simply as 'Ireland', for example in the Good Friday Agreement (1998) (Coakley, 2009).
4 In his satirical novel *Puckoon* (1973), Spike Milligan lampoons the haphazard nature of this particular unruly line.
5 At partition approximately one-third of the population of Northern Ireland was Irish Catholic and two-thirds Ulster Protestant. The 2010 census revealed that 45 per cent of the population was Irish Catholic while 48 per cent was Ulster Protestant. Since then, the gap between the 'two communities' has narrowed further while the percentage of non-aligned has increased.
6 Architects, planners, economists, lawyers, psychologists, historians, creative writers, and electronic engineers have also made important contributions to the body of knowledge on borders and bordering.

7 https://hansard.parliament.uk/Commons/1920-03-29/debates/efde3e8f-5493-4119-9e20–6937a86e2f78/GovernmentOfIrelandBill (accessed 04/05/2020).
8 www.legislation.gov.uk/ukpga/1920/67/pdfs/ukpga_19200067_en.pdf (accessed 04/05/2020).
9 www.difp.ie/docs/1922/Collins-Craig-agreement/226.htm (accessed 04/05/2020).
10 Whyte also detailed many organisations, particularly charitable and welfare organisations and professional associations, that were organised on an east–west (British–Irish) basis, for example the Royal National Lifeboat Institution and the Association of Certified Accountants.
11 The exception was a small number of 'Concession Roads' on which vehicles could travel from one part of a jurisdiction, pass through another jurisdiction, and re-enter the original jurisdiction without stopping.
12 www.irishborderlands.com/living/smuggling/index.html (accessed 10/09/2018).
13 www.irishborderlands.com/living/smuggling/index.html (accessed 10/09/2018).
14 www.irishborderlands.com/living/roadclosures/index.html (accessed 29/01/2020).

2 Debordering|State

Introduction

The index of debordering is the dismantlement of physical border infrastructure (customs posts, security and inspection points, associated armaments, and technological apparatus), the dispersal of border security personnel, and the development of intergovernmental and cross-border cooperation. Europeanisation and the Irish Peace Process have been the twin processes for debordering on the island of Ireland from the early 1990s.

The 1986 Single European Act was the key milestone in reconfiguring member state borders from 'hard' tariff and security barriers to 'soft', open economic bridges. This debordering was required to facilitate the 'four freedoms' of the incoming EU – the free flow of goods, capital, services, and people – and thus operationalise the European Single Market from 31 December 1992 (Anderson and Bort, 2001).

In the specific island-of-Ireland context, debordering was signalled by the British–Irish commitment to intergovernmental cooperation that was first cemented by the 1985 Anglo-Irish Agreement. In addition to the impact of Europeanisation on the Irish border, debordering was further advanced by the 1998 Good Friday Agreement and its establishment of North–South cooperation as a central element of the accord.

Institutionally, the 1998 agreement is most closely associated with the Irish nationalist/Ulster British unionist/'Other'[1] and the Northern Ireland power-sharing Executive and Assembly. However, the institutional framework of governance delivered by the agreement extended beyond the territory of Northern Ireland. It provided for a trans-state North South Ministerial Council, Secretariat, and Implementation Bodies for the island of Ireland, as well as the British–Irish Intergovernmental Conference for inter-state (UK–Ireland) cooperation on non-devolved matters relating to Northern Ireland and a trans-state, trans-regional British–Irish Council. Regarding the debordering of the island of Ireland, the development potential of the

North South Ministerial Council was of particular interest in the aftermath of the agreement.

The argument of this chapter is that debordering the Irish border was initiated by Europeanisation and advanced by the creation of a North–South institutional infrastructure provided by the 1998 agreement. However, it also considers resistance to debordering by newly empowered Ulster British unionists which had the effect of atrophying the main North–South institution, the North South Ministerial Council.

Europeanisation

The concept of Europeanisation encapsulates multifarious understandings of the impact of European integration on a wide breadth of institutions, processes, and interests. It encompasses the state, the region, borders, law, politics and policies, political ideology, migration, society, culture, citizenship, and identities. For Knill (2001, p. 1), Europeanisation is essentially about 'how European integration affects domestic administrative practices and structures'. Featherstone and Radaelli (2003) were also concerned with political aspects of Europeanisation, that is the impact of European integration on member state institutions, administrations, and policies. Richardson (2006) concentrated on the Europeanisation of public policy. Meanwhile, in the legal sphere, the effects of European integration on national law is, naturally, the main interest (Snyder, 2000).

Borneman and Fowler view Europeanisation from the perspective of identities, interpreting it as a concept that refers to the re-organisation of territoriality and 'peoplehood', with consequences for group identification, principally nationhood (1997, p. 487). Spohn and Triandafyllidou (2003) also considered the Europeanisation of collective identities, although their focus was on the particular processes of EU enlargement and migration. Meanwhile, Coman, Kostera, and Tomini (2014) have challenged assumptions of Europeanisation as European identity-building. For Dell'Olio (2005) Europeanisation encapsulates the tension between immigration and citizenship in light of a nascent European citizenship.

Shore used Europeanisation to draw attention to the ways in which EU policy makers have attempted to influence the 're-writing of history,' under the remit of 'cultural action', within the processes of EU polity-building and European identity construction (2000, pp. 56–62). Delanty and Rumford (2005) addressed issues of nation and state as they relate to the re-ordering of European society and societies. The clash between Europeanisation and English nationalism was captured by Tournier-Sol and Gifford (2015), and the one between Europeanisation and Eurosceptic/Europhobe political forces in Central East European member states was considered by Havlik, Hloušek, and Kaniok (2017).

These multifarious interpretations and approaches to Europeanisation underscore the difficulties in defining it as an analytical category in social science. These difficulties motivated Robert Harmsen and Thomas M. Wilson to conduct an audit of the ways in which Europeanisation is understood in research and writing on EU economics, politics, society, and culture. Their audit detailed the multiple usages of the term, from Europeanisation as 'the reconstruction of identities' to narrower policy adaptations within member states to those focused on the reconfiguration of EU governance (2000, pp. 14–7).

The 1986 Single European Act provided for the completion of the Single European Market by 1992 and presented an accelerant for the conceptual development of Europeanisation as an analytical category. The ensuing legal, economic, political, and cultural processes of Europeanisation began to pose serious questions for state sovereignty and the manifestation of state borders as barriers to the free movement of goods, capital, services, and people. Europeanisation confronted the legal and economic sovereignty of the national/nation-state. The EU, delivered by the Maastricht Treaty (1992), presented an overt challenge to its political sovereignty. Member states either embraced or acquiesced in this transference or 'pooling' of sovereignty in response to the contemporary economic, political, and social challenges of globalisation (Sørensen, 1999; Laffan, O'Donnell, and Smith, 2000; Wallace, 2000).

After 1985, there was a dramatic increase in the frequency of EC/EU Intergovernmental Conferences (IGCs) which resulted in a frenetic bout of EC/EU constitution-building. IGC treaty-making resulted in changing the decision-making rules that enabled the EC/EU to increase its policy-making capacity. Consequently, the entrepreneurial EC, led by its proactive president, Jacques Delors, moved the EC/EU into key areas of state activity and highlighted the fact that Europeanisation was reconfiguring West European borders (Caporaso, 1996; Laffan, O'Donnell, and Smith, 2000).

Ireland and the UK in the European embrace

Ireland and the UK acceded to the EC in 1973. After their accession, the relationship between the British and Irish governments began to mature. The old 'cold war' relationship between the two governments, marked by political hostility and Irish economic dependence on British markets, gradually gave way to a new one based on a loosening of Ireland's economic shackles and intergovernmental cooperation between nominally equal member states. EC membership enabled the Irish economy to diversify and expand to European markets, thus reducing its dependence on British markets. Paradoxically, becoming an EC member state and the 'pooling of sovereignty' that it entailed boosted the statehood of Ireland, a former constituent part of the UK, especially in the context of its relationship with its former colonial master (Arthur, 2000, p. 129; O'Ceallaigh and Kilcourse, 2013; O'Leary, 2019a).

Crucially, the EC gave the reconfigured British/Irish relationship space to breathe. British and Irish politicians and civil servants regularly escaped from the claustrophobic territorial confines of past and present British–Irish political conflict (Kelly, 2019). Bilateral British/Irish meetings became commonplace on the fringes of EC/EU meetings in Brussels and Strasbourg, particularly European Council meetings which involved the Irish Taoiseach and the British prime minister. Top of the agenda for these meetings was the Northern Ireland conflict and bilateral approaches to its transformation (McCall, 2001; Murphy, 2016).

Although bilateral summit meetings, beginning in 1980, strengthened the British–Irish intergovernmental relationship serious disagreements were encountered. For instance, the two governments had radically different perspectives on the 1981 Irish Republican Hunger Strike and the 1982 Argentinean invasion of the Falklands/Malvinas. However, in December 1984, British prime minister Margaret Thatcher and Irish Taoiseach Garret FitzGerald met at an EC summit in Dublin. The meeting reopened a line of communication between British and Irish officials responsible for developing the British–Irish intergovernmental relationship (Guelke, 1988, p. 217). Peter Barry (Irish minister for foreign affairs, 1982–7) confirmed the importance of the European space for British–Irish intergovernmental development: '[I]t was only when we both joined the European Union we started to mix with one another both socially and politically' (John Whyte Oral Archive, 2007, p. 20). He continued: '[T]he European Union gave us the platform; it gave us the forum with which we could discuss matters. . . . I can't work out how we would have done it without the European Union' (ibid., p. 23). Paul Murphy (minister of state for Northern Ireland, 1997–9) also credited the EU with providing the context for change in the British–Irish intergovernmental relationship (2019, p. 95).[2]

The first substantive product of this intergovernmental engagement was the 1985 Anglo-Irish Agreement. That seminal agreement gave the Irish government an ill-specified 'less than joint authority, more than consultation' role in Northern Ireland governance (Coakley and Todd, 2020, p. 153). British prime minister Margaret Thatcher's primary motive for signing the agreement was to increase security cooperation. However, the need to place security in the context of a political framework that included an 'Irish dimension' was impressed on the prime minister by ministerial colleagues and civil servants (Goodhall, 1993). While the British government retained constitutional sovereignty over Northern Ireland, the Anglo-Irish Agreement gave the Irish government a shadowing role in the governance of Northern Ireland. In effect, the 1985 agreement established an asymmetrical British–Irish intergovernmental framework for Northern Ireland conflict transformation governance (McLoughlin, 2016). Ulster British unionist and Irish nationalist political parties in Northern Ireland were not formally included in that framework.

The Ulster British response to the Anglo-Irish Agreement

Through the 1985 Anglo-Irish Agreement, the British–Irish intergovernmental relationship began to bear fruit, much to the chagrin of Ulster British unionist leaders in Northern Ireland. The Ulster British unionist myth of being 'under siege' was keenly felt by unionists left powerless in the face of the imposition of this international agreement (Aughey, 1989). For the rest of the 1980s, unionists invested their political energies in an 'Ulster Says No' campaign that ultimately proved fruitless.

By the end of the 1980s, Ulster British unionists were presented with a blizzard of inter-related political dynamics which militated against their traditional ideological position of exclusion regarding Irish nationalists/republicans in the governance of Northern Ireland and hard state borders, especially the border between Northern Ireland and Ireland. These dynamics included the loss of power in 1972 after 50 years of unionist hegemonic rule in Northern Ireland, the transformed British–Irish intergovernmental relationship after 1973, the development of Europeanisation directly affecting the configuration of borders, and a further shift in unionist–nationalist power relations after the signing of the Anglo-Irish Agreement in 1985. These dynamics determined that an Ulster British unionist strategy based on the exclusion of Irish nationalists and a border that functioned as a barrier to North–South, cross-border cooperation was no longer tenable.

Europeanisation was, however, regarded to be detrimental to Ulster British unionist interests because of its perceived incremental assault on UK state sovereignty. The Europhobia of Ulster British unionist leaders was compounded by the Europhile bent of Irish nationalists represented by the Social Democratic and Labour Party (SDLP). In the 1980s and 1990s, unionist leaders, notably the Reverend Ian Paisley, viewed the articulation of 'post-nationalism' and a 'Europe of the Regions' by the then SDLP leader, John Hume, as a Jesuitical plot to bamboozle unionists and mask Irish nationalist irredentist intent. They interpreted Europeanisation as a cunning weapon in the Irish nationalist anti-partitionist canon. Furthermore, the 1985 Anglo-Irish Agreement, which represented an infringement of political and cultural sovereignty, could be connected to the EC mothership of intergovernmentalism. All of this strengthened the Ulster British unionist aversion to Europeanisation (McCall, 2003).

North–South cooperation

There was a slow dawning about the futility of the 'Ulster Say No' campaign by Ulster British unionist leaders during the early post–Anglo-Irish Agreement years. Engagement in a political process involving Irish nationalist politicians was the only viable route to self-empowerment. Nevertheless, the very notion of political *process* implied a route to an unpalatable destination – borderlessness on the island and an all-Ireland state. The political process clashed with the traditional unionist ideological preference for the 1921–72 *status quo* of unionist hegemonic rule in Northern Ireland. The political process flew in the face of the popular Ulster British mantra 'Not an Inch'[3] which dated from the 1920s (Harris, 1995). Therefore, Ulster British unionist leaders acceptance of the three-strand – Northern Ireland, North–South, East–West – structure for negotiations on future governance did not necessarily translate into the acceptance of a political process, leading to a three-strand structure for governance that included formal North–South cooperation.[4] The Reverend Ian Paisley, then Democratic Unionist Party (DUP) leader, was not yet about to do what he had accused Captain Terrence O'Neill of trying to do 25 years earlier, namely 'go over to the other side'. He and his party colleagues staged numerous walkouts during the negotiations, exiting permanently on the arrival of Sinn Féin representatives into those negotiations.[5]

Despite deep ideological reservations, other Ulster British unionists, led by the Ulster Unionist Party (UUP), remained engaged in negotiations.[6] The negotiations, known as the Multi-party Talks, led to the 1998 agreement involved the main political parties in Northern Ireland (except the DUP) and the British and Irish governments. International diplomacy, emanating principally from the United States, played no small part in its securement (Guelke, 2012). The EU provided an important supranational framework and substantial funding for the conflict transformation process. The 1998 Good Friday Agreement was thus the product of a Herculean collective effort to end a violent conflict that had existed for three decades and claimed the lives of more than 3,600 people.

The 1998 agreement created new institutions for Northern Ireland, namely a consociational (power-sharing) Executive, Assembly, and Civic Forum. It also provided all-Ireland institutions in the form of the North South Ministerial Council, Secretariat, and Implementation Bodies. The

British–Irish Council was established to consider matters shared by regional administrations in Scotland, Wales, Northern Ireland, and the Isles of Man, Jersey, and Guernsey, with the participation of British and Irish ministers. For Northern Ireland, the British–Irish Intergovernmental Conference was potentially powerful because it has involved British and Irish governments for the consideration of non-devolved matters relating to Northern Ireland (Nagle, 2018).[7]

John Hume was the principal architect of the Good Friday Agreement. In his essay 'The Irish Question: A British Problem' (in the Winter 1979/1980 Issue of *Foreign Affairs*), he outlined his design and approach to building an agreement. In the intervening years, he was, effectively, an ex officio member of successive Irish governments, intimately connected to influential Irish American policy-makers, and a leading member of the socialist grouping in the European Parliament. This networking portfolio of national and international political contacts enabled Hume to promote and realise his vision (McLoughlin, 2012).

Signatories to the 1998 agreement[8] observed three principles: inclusivity, whereby Irish nationalists and republicans were brought into the new system of governance, alongside Ulster British unionists and non-aligned 'Others'; trans-state, embodied in structures of governance that reach beyond the territorial border of the UK; and consent, whereby the constitutional position of Northern Ireland in the UK could not be changed without the agreement of the majority of people of Northern Ireland. Article 1, paragraph (ii) of the Good Friday Agreement states that the two governments

> recognise that it is for the people of the island of Ireland alone, by agreement between the two parts respectively and without external impediment, to exercise their right of self-determination on the basis of consent, freely and concurrently given, North and South, to bring about a united Ireland, if that is their wish, accepting that this right must be achieved and exercised with and subject to the agreement and consent of a majority of the people of Northern Ireland.

The precedent set by simultaneous referenda on the Good Friday Agreement, North and South, suggests that the agreement of the people of Ireland to a 'united Ireland' would follow the same path.

The 1998 amendment of Articles 2 and 3 of Bunreacht na hÉireann|Constitution of Ireland had the effect of neutralising the territorial threat for the Ulster British unionist community. While unity remained 'the firm will of the Irish nation', 'respect for diversity of . . . identities and traditions' (revised Article 3.1) intimated that unity does not necessarily mean a unitary state should consent for a 'united Ireland' be forthcoming in the North and in the South (O'Leary, 2001, p. 67).

The agreement's North–South institutions stirred little controversy in the Ulster British unionist community, principally because issues of early prisoner release, police reform, and Irish Republican Army decommissioning were more pressing concerns. In any case, pro-agreement unionist leaders presented the North–South institutions as being strictly under the control of the Northern Ireland Assembly and limited to practical low-level cross-border cooperation. However, their political spin was not helped by the live television broadcast of the inaugural meeting of the North South Ministerial Council in December 1999, particularly the arrival in Armagh, Northern Ireland, of the entire ministerial cabinet of the Irish government in a solemn cavalcade of black Mercedes cars, as if en route to the funeral of Northern Ireland.

While the 1998 agreement reaffirmed UK sovereignty over Northern Ireland in the formal-legal sense the North–South and East–West institutions were clearly geared towards spreading the political and cultural substance of sovereignty across and beyond states (Ruane and Todd, 2001, p. 936). Thus, debordering the Irish border was advanced by the agreement's constitutional ingenuity and its re-imagining of state sovereignty, as well as the emphasis on overcoming borders as barriers to mobility, contact, communication, cooperation, and trade. Debordering was visibly bolstered by the incremental removal of the selective British security regime along the Irish border by the early 2000s.

Together, the launch of the European Single Market in 1992 and the onset of the Irish Peace Process in 1994 meant that border customs posts and border security checkpoint instillations were no longer required. Secondary roads were re-opened and militarised sections of the Irish border gradually became demilitarised through the removal of British Army border checkpoints, the dismantlement of British Army mountaintop watchtowers in South Armagh and the closure of heavily fortified security bases along the border (Nash, Reid, and Graham, 2013, pp. 109–11). The result was that the physical manifestation of the Irish border itself became barely discernible except for a change in road markings and some 'Welcome to Northern Ireland' signs erected by the Northern Ireland Department of Regional Development in 2012, although many of these signs were removed, vandalised, defaced, or, in one instance, riddled with bullet holes.[9]

The continuing insurgent activity of small Irish republican splinter groups in the border region thereafter did little to disrupt debordering. For example, in August 2009, one such group left a 300-kg bomb outside Forkhill, County Armagh, running a concealed command wire across the border into County Louth. A telephone warning was given, but a week passed before

British security forces located the bomb. Upon the discovery, the British government asserted that the British Army would not be re-introduced to secure the Irish border. Ten years later, in August 2019, an explosion near Wattlebridge, County Fermanagh, close to the border with County Cavan, was attributed to a republican splinter group. Again, there was no immediate British government appetite for rebordering the Irish border.[10]

Since the Good Friday Agreement, police cooperation across the Irish border has developed through informal networks and cross-border agreements, although largely without overarching transparent regulatory and accountability structures and processes. Primarily, its focus has been on organised crime and the activities of continuing republican insurgents. One example of this cooperation was the cross-border investigation into the murder of Paul Quinn by a criminal gang south of the border in 2007. An Garda Siochána (Irish Police) and Police Service of Northern Ireland (PSNI) officers operated as a team with Gardai conducting door-to-door enquiries in Northern Ireland (accompanied by PSNI personnel) while PSNI officers attended the interviews of suspects and witnesses in Ireland (Walsh, 2011). An example of organic cross-border cooperation involving Garda and PSNI officers was the prolonged search in 2016 for the body of a young man believed to have drowned in the River Erne which traverses the Irish border. Police and a significant number of people from both sides of the border joined forces in the search that ended after two months when the body was found. In the intervening period, strong bonds of friendship were forged, with one police officer remarking, '[W]e saw these people realising that there is very little actually separating us' (Pollak, 2016).

The North South Ministerial Council

The North South Ministerial Council is the institutional custodian of North–South, cross-border activities and cooperation on the island of Ireland. Composed of members of the Irish government and Northern Ireland Executive, it has been the most significant institutional development in North–South relations since partition. The areas identified for North–South, cross-border cooperation were education – education for children with special needs, educational under-achievement, teacher qualifications and school, youth, and teacher exchanges; health – accident and emergency planning, cooperation on high-technology equipment, cancer research, and health promotion; transport – strategic transport planning for road and rail infrastructure, services, and safety; agriculture – common agricultural policy, animal and plant health policy, and research and rural development; the environment – environmental protection, pollution, water quality management, and waste management; and tourism – the promotion of the island of Ireland overseas as a tourist destination.[11] Underneath broad areas like agriculture, health, and education are specific areas for North–South, cross-border cooperation such as milk production, cancer treatment, and cultural activities for young people. In the specific area contexts, 156 areas of cross-border cooperation were detailed in a *Technical Explanatory Note: North-South Cooperation Mapping Exercise* (Department for Exiting the European Union, 2018) undertaken by the UK and the EU.[12]

Meetings of the North South Ministerial Council have been conducted in plenary, sectoral, and institutional forms. Plenary meetings have involved the Irish Taoiseach, the Northern Ireland first and deputy first ministers, and other ministers from North and South. They are essentially stage-managed political events designed to animate the North–South dimension of the Good Friday Agreement. The sectoral meetings have involved ministers from the North and the South responsible for specific sectors to progress areas of cross-border cooperation under their remits. Institutional meetings have overseen the work undertaken by the North South Implementation Bodies which are responsible for cross-border implementation in the specific areas of food safety, minority languages (Gaelic and Ulster-Scots), trade and business development, aquaculture, waterways, EU programmes, and tourism promotion (Coakley, Ó Caoindealbháin, and Wilson, 2006).

The North South Ministerial Council was allocated a measure of autonomy in pursuit of its goals of cooperation and coordination provided agreement was reached among participants, including Ulster British unionist representatives. However, decisions reached in the council that were 'beyond the authority of those attending' required the consent of both the Oireachtas (Irish Parliament) and the Northern Ireland Assembly (*The Agreement*, Strand 2, para. 6). The initial refusal of Ulster British unionist ministers to attend any North South Ministerial Council meeting that included Sinn Féin members, which was announced on 21 September 2002, highlighted unionist self-empowerment through engagement in the political process, albeit via the power of veto exercised over the development of North–South cooperation.[13]

Thus, despite its institutional manifestation – with imposing headquarters for its Joint Secretariat in Armagh – and the considerable breadth of its remit,[14] the North South Ministerial Council did not enjoy plain sailing. In fact, the political waters were decidedly choppy, pummelling this nascent all-island institution. Three particular challenges arose. First, it has had to endure prolonged periods of suspension because of political disputes surrounding the implementation of the agreement and the governance of Northern Ireland. For example, there were prolonged periods of suspension between 2002 to 2007 and between 2017[15] and 2020.[16] During these periods, Joint Secretariat staff members were redeployed elsewhere in the Irish Civil Service and Northern Ireland Civil Service, with disruptive consequences for continuity and momentum. Second, the Joint Secretariat is responsible for the generation and coordination of cross-border policies. However, there was an imbalance in North–South leadership in that context because Northern Ireland government departments demonstrated a lack of commitment to cross-border development that could inform the work of the Joint Secretariat. Third, and most significant, the DUP remained ideologically opposed to North–South institutionalised cooperation.

DUP leaders characterised the North South Ministerial Council as a waste of money and called for its suspension.[17] While not objecting to low-level cross-border initiatives in the Irish border region, the DUP remained ideologically opposed to any public institution that it perceived to be 'all-Ireland' in remit and operation. The North South Ministerial Council is the institutional embodiment of an all-Ireland approach to governance.

Individual DUP ministers also attempted to frustrate the work of the North South Ministerial Council. For example, in the sectoral context, a DUP minister questioned the need for face-to-face meetings with his Irish government counterpart, citing a concern for the environment. A decade before the COVID-19 pandemic necessitated social distancing, the use of technology was mooted by the DUP minister as a way of circumventing face-to-face contact with southern counterparts.[18]

Arlene Foster (a subsequent DUP leader) articulated the feeling that such North–South institutionalisation contributes to the feeling of threat in the Ulster British community:

> Sometimes if you give it [North–South cooperation] a grand name and give it a grand structure then people rightly feel threatened on some occasions. But if communities are working together [cross-border] in a very low-level way and getting on and making relationships for their own communities then it works. I'm not ruling out having relationships – as one would expect in normal times – between two neighbouring countries, if there is an issue that has to be dealt with by Belfast and Dublin.[19]

This low-level approach is reminiscent of the 'quiet' North–South cooperation of the 1925–59 period identified by Michael Kennedy (2000), except that the DUP's emphasis is on cross-border cooperation corralled within the third (voluntary and community) sector.

The Ulster British unionist approach to debordering through the development of North–South cooperation is informed by their political, economic, social, and cultural understanding of the Irish state. The yardstick of this interpretation is the perceived sense of threat emanating from the South. In 1995, the then UUP MP John D. Taylor (subsequently Lord Kilclooney) embarked on a campaign to secure the leadership of his party. Although beaten to the leadership by David Trimble, Taylor's campaign was remarkable because he talked at venues throughout Ireland, North and South. In his speeches, he concentrated on the remit of proposed North–South institutions. Drawing a distinction between 'cross-border' and 'all-Ireland' references in this context, Taylor argued that the former were acceptable whereas the latter were anathema to Ulster British unionists (Cash, 1996, p. 216). He also emphasised the need for unionists to embark upon a cooperative relationship with the SDLP and the Irish government. Significantly, Taylor sought to challenge the traditional Ulster British unionist interpretation of Ireland as exclusively Catholic and Gaelic when noting 'significant progress towards the creation of a pluralist society free from church control'.[20] Such a challenge signalled the possibility of downgrading the perceived cultural threat emanating from the South. However, opposition to North–South cooperation, rather than cross-border cooperation, has been a constant in the Ulster British unionist position. Therefore, the North South Ministerial Council is the prime target of unionist opposition.

Although hampered by the periodic suspension and 'live' containment of the North South Ministerial Council, the North South Implementation Bodies remained operational throughout. They concentrate on specific areas of cross-border cooperation including trade and business development, inland waterways, food safety, the Irish and Ulster-Scots languages, agriculture and marine matters, and special EU programmes. The most significant North South Implementation Body is the Special EU Programmes Body (SEUPB). It was given responsibility for the management of the EU Peace II (2000–6) programme and the Interreg IIIA programme (2000–6) in Ireland, as well as their successors.

With its wide-ranging and complex mandate regarding structural funds and community initiatives, as well as limited staff and resources, the SEUPB faced a number of challenges regarding its ability to balance management and development and all-island and cross-border aspects, as well as its novel trans-state position in a multilevel network stretching from the local grassroots level to the supranational EU level (Laffan and Payne, 2001, pp. 14–5). Perhaps because of administrative difficulties and structural complexity, the SEUPB initially relied on the Northern Ireland Department of Finance and Personnel for support in the exercise of its managerial authority.

There is no doubt that political crises in the implementation of the 1998 agreement seriously impeded innovation and development regarding North–South cooperation. Indeed, the North South Ministerial Council emerged as a first port of call for the exercise of the Ulster British unionist veto when difficulties were experienced. There were also predictable problems involving staff and resource transfer and the shift of responsibility from central administrations to the novel trans-state Implementation Bodies. Consequently, Ulster British unionist resistance, institutional change, and funding difficulties posed serious challenges for debordering the island of Ireland.

Conclusion

Debordering is characterised by the dismantlement of physical border infrastructure, the dispersal of border security personnel, and intergovernmental and cross-border cooperation. Europeanisation and the Irish Peace Process brought debordering to the island of Ireland in the 1990s.

The development of British–Irish intergovernmental cooperation was facilitated by the joint accession of Ireland and the UK to the EC in 1973. Eventually, it produced the 1985 Anglo-Irish Agreement which gave the Irish government 'a say' in Northern Ireland public affairs, especially those related to conflict transformation. The 1998 Good Friday Agreement established North–South cooperation institutionally. In addition to its provision of the Irish nationalist/Ulster British unionist/non-aligned 'Other' Northern Ireland power-sharing Executive and Assembly, the agreement created a trans-state, North South Ministerial Council, Secretariat, and Implementation Bodies for the island of Ireland. It also delivered the British-Irish Intergovernmental Conference for intergovernmental (UK–Ireland) cooperation on non-devolved issues relating to Northern Ireland and a trans-state, trans-regional British–Irish Council. In the context of debordering on the island of Ireland, the North South Ministerial Council has been the key institution.

Despite the substantial problems, 'live' North–South institutions remained pivotal to the progress of debordering. Consensual North and South, Irish nationalist and Ulster British unionist decision-making is a baseline necessity for debordering through North–South cooperation. In practical terms, it involved the attendance of two northern ministers, one with sectoral responsibility and a 'shadow minister' from the other (Irish nationalist or Ulster British unionist) community, at every sectoral North South Ministerial Council meeting (Pollak, 2001, p. 16). The practical operation of North–South institutions, relatively free from political symbolism, enabled Ulster British unionists to acquiesce in the operation of North–South cooperation. The sufficient easing of conflict between unionists and nationalists, resulting from an ideological shift on the part of nationalist/republican and pro-agreement unionist leaders, was central to this endeavour.

When past failures and the ongoing Irish/Ulster British political and cultural conflict is considered, it is something of an extraordinary achievement that North–South cooperation was institutionalised and operated, if not continuously and easily. However, it was the Good Friday Agreement's empowerment of Ulster British unionist leaders, and their subsequent resistance to North–South cooperation, that helped atrophy the North South Ministerial Council.

Notes

1 The 'Others' are those not aligned to the Ulster British unionist and Irish nationalist communal blocs. Their political parties include the Alliance Party of Northern Ireland, the Green Party for Northern Ireland, and People Before Profit.
2 I am grateful to my PhD student, Darren Litter, for drawing my attention to these testimonies.
3 https://cain.ulster.ac.uk/othelem/glossary.htm#N (accessed 05/04/2020).
4 Strand 1 – Northern Ireland; Strand 2 – island of Ireland; Strand 3 – Britain and Ireland.
5 Sinn Féin joined the multi-party negotiations in September 1994 after the Irish Republican Army ceasefire.
6 However, there were a number of high-profile defections from the UUP to the DUP during negotiations, notably Jeffery Donaldson and Arlene Foster (a future leader of the DUP).
7 Provision for the nominal inclusion of non-governmental participants, by means of consultation, was also made through the establishment of a Civic Forum as part of the agreement's infrastructure (McCall and Williamson, 2001). However, this branch eventually withered on the new governance tree.
8 Those signing up to (although not physically signing) the 1998 Good Friday Agreement included the British and Irish governments, the leaders of the UUP, the SDLP, Sinn Féin, and the Alliance Party, as well as those from more minor political parties. The DUP walked out of multi-party talks and subsequently formally rejected the agreement.
9 The latter at the border crossing between Ballyconnell, County Cavan (Ireland) and Derrylin, County Fermanagh (Northern Ireland). See www.irishnews.com/news/brexit/2017/12/08/news/brexit-border-assurances-are-politically-bulletproof-says-taoiseach-leo-varadkar-1206145/(accessed 08/07/2019).
10 www.psni.police.uk/news/Latest-News/220819-update-on-the-explosion-in-the-wattlebridge-area/ (accessed 22/08/2019).
11 www.northsouthministerialcouncil.org/index/areas-of-co-operation.htm (accessed 27/12/2019).
12 https://assets.publishing.service.gov.uk/government/uploads/system/uploads/attachment_data/file/762820/Technical_note-_North-South_cooperation_mapping_exercise__2_.pdf (accessed 15/12/2019).
13 David Trimble (then UUP leader and Northern Ireland first minister) had imposed a previous ban on the participation of Sinn Féin ministers in North South Ministerial Council meetings.
14 Prior to one prolonged suspension of the agreement's main institutions in 2002, the North South Ministerial Council began to address the potentially important issue of opening a vertical line of communication to the EC regarding North–South interests. While the Northern Ireland Assembly was bound by its devolved status from entering into international relations, the Northern Ireland Act (1998) did not withhold 'the exercise of legislative powers so far as required for giving effect to any agreement or arrangement entered into' (Section 55)

in the North South Ministerial Council or by or in relation to the North South Implementation Bodies (Hadfield, 2001, p. 97). Thus, legally, the North–South institutions were free to conduct their trans-state operations on an all-island and an EU-wide basis. These legislative powers were facilitated by the ambiguous article in the 1998 agreement which states, 'Arrangements to be made to ensure that the views of the [North South Ministerial] Council are taken into account and represented appropriately at relevant EU meetings' (Strand 2, para. 17). As such, it had the potential to be a novel institutional cog in EU governance. Politically, however, this was an imaginative leap too far.

15 This prolonged suspension was a direct result of 'Stormontgate' which began with a PSNI (police) raid on the Sinn Féin offices at Parliament Buildings, Stormont, in October 2002. Documents and computers were seized, and three workers were arrested on suspicion of subversive activity. Charges against the three were dropped in December 2005, and one of the three, Denis Donaldson, head of the Sinn Féin offices at Parliament Buildings, subsequently admitted to being a British spy. He was shot dead in April 2006.

16 The suspension between January 2017 and January 2020 was the result of a disagreement between the DUP and Sinn Féin across a range of issues, including a corruption scandal, abortion rights, and same-sex marriage.

17 *Irish Times*, 02/01/2009 and 10/02/2009.

18 *Belfast Telegraph*, 19/03/2010.

19 Interview, 20/05/2007.

20 *Irish Times* 02/03/1995.

3 Debordering|Communities

Introduction

Underneath the institutional architecture of North–South cooperation a living Irish cultural borderscape denoted by debordering, long-term peacebuilding, and conflict transformation emerged. The EU has been integral to the development of this borderscape through its provision of funding for cross-border, cross-community (Irish/Ulster British) partnerships, principally through the EU Peace programmes for Northern Ireland and the border counties of Ireland (from 1995). This 'grassroots' cross-border cooperation, most closely associated with the third (voluntary and community) sector, has been important for sustaining and developing debordering, long-term peacebuilding, and conflict transformation, especially when the political process was in abeyance.

Borderscapes have been interpreted as sites of cultural and political complexity, contestation, and struggles over inclusion and exclusion (Rajaram and Grundy-Warr, 2008, pp. ix–xi). However, a very different interpretation posits borderscapes as enablers of mobility, contact, communication, and cooperation. Chiara Brambilla maintains that 'the borderscapes concept is mainly inscribed in the opportunity of liberating political imagination from the burden of the territorialist imperative while opening up spaces within which the organization of new forms of the political and the social become possible' (2015, p. 112). EU borderscapes may be viewed as potential liberating spaces for intercultural contact, communication, and cooperation that interrogate binary distinctions between 'self' and 'other', 'us' and 'them', 'friends' and 'enemies', 'here' and 'there', 'home' and 'abroad', 'domestic' and 'foreign', 'threat' and 'security', and 'include' and 'exclude'.

The act of crossing the border itself presents challenges to cultural, political, and social meanings, as well as opportunities for examining alternatives. Borderscapes embody the fact that political, social, and cultural dynamics stray well beyond the 'line in the sand'. Borderscapes may, therefore, be construed as gateways, areas of opportunities, zones of contact, communication and cooperation, and if not ambivalent identities, then self-reflexive ones.

Liam O'Dowd concedes that such concepts or metaphors are essential for scientific analysis but cautions against overextending them (2010, p. 1038). While heeding O'Dowd's advice, this chapter mobilises the borderscape concept and applies it to the multitude of EU Peace programme initiatives centred on cross-border, cross-community cooperation on the island of Ireland.

Under the auspices of EU Peace programmes cross-border projects in the Irish cultural borderscape mushroomed during the 1990s. They provided the island's Irish and Ulster British communities with opportunities for contact, communication, and cooperation that challenged binary territorial identity distinctions, explored cultural commonality as well as diversity, and built cross-border, cross-community relationships that advanced long-term peacebuilding and conflict transformation on the island of Ireland. Sports, history, and languages have been cultural resources for creating opportunities for cross-border, cross-community contact, communication, and cooperation.

Can borderscapes that emphasise borders as gateways, areas of opportunities, zones of mobility, contact, communication, and cooperation engender inclusionary diversions in Irish nationalism and Ulster British unionism/nationalism that advance long-term peacebuilding and conflict transformation? This chapter argues that an inclusionary Irish cultural borderscape presented a robust local-level, 'grassroots' model for long-term peacebuilding and conflict transformation on the island of Ireland.

Borderscapes as peace projects

The 'founding fathers' of European integration – Konrad Adenauer, Joseph Bech, Johan Willem Beyen, Alcide De Gasperi, Jean Monnet, Robert Schuman, Paul-Henri Spaak, and Altiero Spinelli – had to accept the outcome of war in Europe and the borders it had drawn. However, their twin objectives of economic regeneration and peacebuilding after World War II eventually determined that European integration would entail a reconfiguration of Europe's 'hard borders' to 'soft borders'. 'Hard borders' as high-tariff barriers impeded European economic development. 'Hard borders' as physical barriers also hindered the contact, communication, and cooperation across borders that benefit a long-term peacebuilding enterprise. Intergovernmentalism and cross-border cooperation are the inter-related processes that have helped to reconfigure the borders of member states committed to European integration.

The Franco-German intergovernmental relationship was sealed by German chancellor Helmut Köhl and French president François Mitterrand during their meeting on 22 September 1984 at the site of the First World War Battle of Verdun to commemorate the dead of the two World Wars. This highly symbolic meeting emphasised peacebuilding through European integration after the devastation of war in Europe. The Council of Europe sponsored cross-border cooperation from the 1950s was an important local and regional forerunner to this symbolic event. Such regional and local cross-border cooperation, including that between Danish and German regional authorities, as well as Franco-German youth exchanges beginning in the 1950s, began to build the peace from the bottom up (Pollak, 2011).

Yet, three decades of EU sponsored cross-border cooperation produced underwhelming results in progressing peacebuilding throughout European borderscapes. The communicative symbolism of cross-border cooperation has all too rarely translated into intercultural interaction across borderscapes. Partly, this stems from the lack of deep and sustained support for intercultural cross-border cooperation projects that have peacebuilding as a central theme. Cross-border projects are primarily economic and/or security in orientation with the promotion of intercultural dialogue an afterthought. Few cross-border projects have directly confronted the legacy of border conflict and the residual emotions of suspicion, fear, resentment, grievance, and hatred left in its wake (Berezin, 2003; MacMillan, 2020).

Conflict emotions can provide the inspiration for 'normal people' to contemplate killing other people. Emotion entrepreneurs can stir conflict emotions and create the conditions for political mobilisation in pursuit of conflict. These emotions can also swell of their own volition when shifts in the balance of power or in the demographic relationship with the 'Significant Other' become disadvantageous. Fear inhabits frightened minds, resentment appears in glistening eyes, hatred occupies hardened hearts, and love for comrades and country, to the exclusion of all others, becomes all-consuming.

The residue of conflict emotions, still felt in some borderscapes, may provide the motivation for avoiding cross-border contact, communication, and cooperation. German and Polish borderlanders are more likely to shun contact than engage with 'the Other' across the border (Stokłosa, 2014). The Three-Borders Area of Austria, Italy, and Slovenia remains hard bordered in the imaginations of borderlanders, with each region fixed firmly on their state centre and away from the border (Janschitz and Kofler, 2004). In the Carpathian Euroregion, cross-border cooperation exacerbated anti-Ukrainian sentiment (Hann, 1998, p. 254). In Hungarian/Romanian Euroregions, different competencies on either side of the border contributed to animosity between Hungarian and Romanian local officials. Meanwhile, here as elsewhere, ordinary borderlanders remained unaware of cross-border 'Euroregions' and their purpose (Szabó and Koncz, 2006, pp. 165–70; Erőss et al., 2011, p. 82). Temporary physical rebordering within the EU, in response to the Mediterranean migration crisis peaking in 2015, provided a confirming physical manifestation of these borders of the imagination.

In such cases, EU attempts to promote cross-border cooperation can smack of insensitivity and arrogance. However, the provenance, size, complexity, and range of borderscapes throughout Europe vary greatly, and it should not be assumed that the lack of appetite for cross-border cooperation in some borderscapes and among some borderlanders is replicated in all borderscapes and among all borderlanders (McCall, 2014). If fortune favours and appetites are whetted then, there are possibilities for peacebuilding through the re-evaluation of national histories and the re-examination of national identities.

Borderscapes are cultural spaces that can embody the integrative symbolism of European integration. Cross-border cooperation initiatives in borderscapes may generate mobility, contact, communication, and cooperation that can help address and transform conflict issues. Understanding the cultural position of the 'Significant Other' and respecting cultural differences is key to progressing peacebuilding in borderscapes. Cross-border symbolic enterprises, including bilingual or multilingual place names and street signs and public space art, can reflect the peacebuilding ideal of a shared borderscape space. The level of popular involvement in cross-border cooperation projects is a core determinant of their worth for long-term peacebuilding and conflict transformation.

Debordering and conflict transformation

Cordula Reimann determined that 'conflict transformation refers to outcome, process and structure oriented long-term peacebuilding efforts, which aim to truly overcome revealed forms of direct cultural and structural violence' (2004, p. 51). Conflict transformation involves a long-term peacebuilding project wherein political violence has abated, appropriate structures of governance have been established, competing political elites – 'the treetops' – have entered into an agreement on governance and, crucially, local communities – 'the grassroots' – have been engaged in long-term peacebuilding (Ramsbotham, Woodhouse, and Miall, 2011, p. 244).

Accordingly, conflict transformation captures Irish/Ulster British long-term peacebuilding wherein political violence largely abated, appropriate structures of governance were created by the 1998 Good Friday Agreement (including North–South institutions), competing Ulster British unionist and Irish nationalist political parties entered into the agreement on governance, and local Irish and Ulster British 'grassroots' communities engaged in a peacebuilding process. It is now generally accepted by peacebuilding theorists that the engagement of 'the grassroots', long advocated by John Paul Lederach (1995, p. 26), is a key component of long-term peacebuilding.

Debordering communities rests on cross-border contact, communication, and cooperation. The outcomes of this contact, communication, and cooperation include cross-border institutional and policy development, cross-border economic initiatives with mutually beneficial outcomes, and cross-border community development and cultural interaction. Emmanuelle Brunet-Jailly considered the importance of the culture of borderscape communities in determining a border's dividing or bridging capacity (Brunet-Jailly, 2005, pp. 638–9). Their cultures can militate against the bridging impetus of EU cross-border cooperation initiatives. For example, the decades-long blossoming of multiple Euroregions across the German–Polish border resulted in economic, transport, and environmental dividends. Between 1994 and 2006, €400 million was channelled into the Polish–German cross-border cooperation programme for improving cross-border roads and environmental protection (Scott, 2011, p. 124). However, German and Polish borderlanders have generally avoided cross-border cultural interaction. This is a borderscape that is informed by contested discourses and meanings and struggles over inclusion and exclusion. The persistence of an imagined German–Polish border and exclusionary mentalities forged in the fires of twentieth-century wars explain the lack of cross-border interaction. Accordingly, two-thirds of German–Polish borderlanders see themselves as either 'neutral' or 'unfriendly' towards their neighbours on the other side of the border (Gorzelak, 2006, pp. 200–4).

Katarzyna Stokłosa confirmed that the German/Polish border is imagined as a hard border by many German and Polish borderlanders. Stokłosa acknowledges the existence of high levels of cross-border interaction in some areas, notably, cross-border shopping. However, for conflict transformation, the value of shopping is questionable not least because of the limited social engagement and cultural interaction involved in cruising the aisles of a supermarket. Few German or Polish borderlanders claim cross-border friendships. Moreover, German stereotypes of Poles as lazy, car thieves, and criminals and Polish stereotypes of Germans as 'Nazis' persist (Stokłosa, 2014, pp. 263–71). There were also signs of a deterioration in the German/Polish intergovernmental relationship after the election of Polish Eurosceptic Law and Justice Party in October 2014 (Nougayrède, 2016). This did not augur well for the future development German/Polish conflict transformation if, as argued here and elsewhere (McCall, 2014), an intergovernmental cooperation framework is necessary for 'grassroots' cross-border cooperation as conflict transformation.

When considering stubborn borders of the imagination it is tempting to accept the view that the production of cross-border zones of contact, communication, and cooperation has deleterious consequences for some borderscapes where borderlanders on either side of a border shun contact, communication, and cooperation across it. They give succour to David Newman's (2006, pp. 180–1) claim that the EU's creation of cross-border zones of contact, communication, and cooperation is artificial. However, experiences differ widely throughout the EU's borderscapes. Some can display cultural and political complexity, contested discourses and meanings, and struggles over inclusion and exclusion. Others can be configured as networks that enable flows of mobility, contact, communication, and cooperation. One has only to contrast the large, relatively hostile German/Polish borderscape with the much smaller, 'friendly borderscape' shared by Denmark and Germany (Klatt and Herrmann, 2011). Consequently, where welcome, cross-border cooperation in a borderscape can open up political, social, and cultural spaces in which national histories are re-examined, the configuration of national identities re-evaluated, and nationalisms rendered accommodatory (O'Dowd, Anderson, and Wilson, 2003).

The Irish cultural borderscape and conflict transformation

By the 1990s, numerous factors had gained sufficient traction to persuade political parties in Northern Ireland to move from conflict towards conflict transformation. These included the ending of the British/Irish 'cold war' through the development of a British/Irish intergovernmental relationship after both states joined the EEC in 1973; the 1985 Anglo-Irish Agreement which gave the Irish government an advisory role in the governance of Northern Ireland; the impact of European integration on member state's sovereignty and borders; demographic change through a numerically strengthening Irish national community in Northern Ireland; the subsequent re-articulation of Irish nationalism; the violent stalemate between Irish republican insurgents, Ulster British loyalist paramilitaries, and the British Army, recognised by all sides after two decades of violence; and the subsequent paramilitary ceasefires of 1994. The changing international context after the collapse of communism and the 11 September 2001 Islamist jihadist attacks on the US persuaded the Irish Republican Army (IRA) leadership to commit wholly to 'political struggle' and jettison a 'violent liberation struggle' ideology once shared with the African National Congress, the Palestine Liberation Organization, and Euskadi Ta Askatasuna/Basque Homeland and Liberty (McCall, 2001).

An Irish cultural borderscape for conflict transformation began to flourish in the 1990s. The EU has been the key generator of this Irish borderscape. Debordering, through the removal of border customs posts after the introduction of the European Single Market on 31 December 1992, cleared the way for an Irish cultural borderscape to develop. That development was supported by cross-border, cross-community cooperation initiatives mostly funded by the EU's Interreg and Peace programmes (Lagana, 2021). From 1989, the EU-wide Interreg programme supported regional-, city-, and local-level cross-border cooperation to promote debordering and erode 'from below' administrative, political, cultural, social, and emotional obstacles to the creation and functioning of the Single Market (Phinnemore and McGowan, 2013, p. 304). Peacebuilding is not an Interreg programme priority though borderscape peacebuilding across the EU may be regarded as a by-product of such cross-border cooperation. The Ireland-specific EU Peace programmes (from 1995) are directly focused on conflict transformation and long-term peacebuilding.

The Peace I programme (1995–9) received €500 million in EU funding, with the British and Irish governments contributing an additional €167 million. Between 2000 and 2004, Peace II secured €531 million from the EU and €304 million from the two governments. Peace II was extended to 2006, with €160 million in total funding: €78 million from the EU and €82 million from the two governments. Peace III (2007–13) accounted for €225 million from the EU and €108 million from the two governments. Peace IV (2014–20) funding amounted to €229 million from the EU and €41 million from the two governments. In total, from 1995 to 2020, the Peace programmes have provided €2,265 million for long-term peacebuilding and conflict transformation.[1] Fifteen per cent of both Peace I and Peace II funding was designated for a cross-border cooperation priority. Cross-border cooperation continued as a 'cross-cutting theme' in Peace III and Peace IV.[2]

The EU-wide Interreg programmes supported cross-border cooperation in an attempt to offset the negative effects of EU economic integration for peripheral regions.[3] In Ireland, they are most closely associated with financing the re-opening of cross-border roads and bridges that had been rendered impassable during the decades of bordering. Overall, the Peace and Interreg programmes resulted in tens of thousands of infrastructural, economic, environmental, educational, training, social, cultural, and other projects (Pollak, 2011). They helped create an Irish cultural borderscape as an inclusionary scape for contact, communication, and cooperation aimed at long-term peacebuilding and conflict transformation.

From an Ulster British unionist perspective, the diminishing political and violent threats from Irish nationalism and republicanism, respectively, lessened the significance of the Irish border as a symbol of threat and insecurity.

Consequently, the Irish borderscape offered a less contentious space in which Irish and Ulster British incompatibilities could be addressed and cultural differences and commonalities explored through local 'grassroots' community contact, communication, and cooperation.

Ulster British 'grassroots' groups were slow to become involved in cross-border activities funded under Peace I (1995–9). However, the optimism generated by the 1998 Good Friday Agreement helped boost Ulster British confidence and involvement under Peace II (2000–6). Indeed, some Ulster British group leaders stated a preference for cross-border projects rather than cross-community projects within Northern Ireland. They reasoned that the Irish national community south of the border represented a less threatening Irish national 'Other' because they were outside the territorial cage of the Northern Ireland conflict. Nevertheless, some also stated that cross-border cooperation was a necessary precursor to Irish/Ulster-British cross-community contact, communication, and cooperation in Northern Ireland which remained largely segregated territorially[4] (O'Dowd and McCall, 2008, pp. 81–99).

The Irish cultural borderscape provided opportunities for escaping the territorial cage of conflict in Northern Ireland, thus underpinning and advancing conflict transformation. The Irish cultural borderscape resonates with the idea of borders being reconfigured as networks that increasingly enable flows of mobility, contact, communication, and cooperation (Rumford, 2006, p. 55). The borders-as-networks thesis is undermined by the twenty-first-century turn in international relations that looks to border security to curtail the movement of would-be international terrorists, criminals, and contested migrants (Vaughan-Williams, 2009). However, by this point, a border security regime for the Irish border was a thing of the past.

EU Peace programmes' cross-border cooperation projects

Through its Peace programmes for Northern Ireland and the border counties of Ireland, the EU endeavoured to support political efforts dedicated to accommodating political and cultural differences and transcending ingrained territoriality. The Peace programmes helped create cross-border networks for contact, communication, and cooperation among people on either side of the border. These networks of contact, communication, and cooperation were made manifest in cross-border, cross-community partnerships funded by the Peace programmes. It has been estimated that more than 161,000 people participated in cross-border, cross-community activities sponsored by Peace II (2000–6) alone.[5] Between 1995 and 2008, 450,000 individuals had participated in EU Peace and Interreg funded projects[6] – a very high level of participation from a population of approximately 2.5 million in Northern Ireland and the border counties of Ireland (Buchanan, 2014).

In Peace programme projects, Ulster British and Irish differences and commonalities have been explored at a local community level through contact, communication, and cooperation on a cross-border, cross-community basis. The communication aspect is an important consideration because language does not just inform but because it may also impact emotions, something that is integral to conflict transformation where residual conflict emotions require remedial work (Britton, 2000). The communication that thousands upon thousands of EU Peace programme projects have facilitated a loosening of the shackles of binary distinctions between 'self' and 'other', 'us' and 'them', 'friends' and 'enemies', 'here' and 'there', 'home' and 'abroad', 'domestic' and 'foreign', 'threat' and 'security', and 'include' and 'exclude'. Those binary distinctions had been forged by bordering from 1921. They were hardened further by decades of violent conflict after 1969, mainly in Northern Ireland but also spilling over the border on occasion.

Advances in the Irish Peace Process and institutionalised North–South cooperation on the island of Ireland were important for Irish cultural borderscape development. The 1998 Good Friday Agreement's provision of cross-border institutions was the key infrastructural element. After the agreement, the Special EU Programmes Body (SEUPB), one of the North South Implementation Bodies attached to the North South Ministerial Council, was given responsibility for the management of the Peace II programme, as well as Interreg IIIA and their successors.

Ramsbotham, Woodhouse, and Miall have written that 'while much literature on peacebuilding agrees with the desirability of approaches involving peacebuilding from below, practical ways of engaging in this process are often lacking' (2011, p. 355). On the island of Ireland, the EU Peace programmes produced a wealth of projects that redress this gap between peacebuilding theory and practice.

EU Peace programme projects have challenged stereotypes and explored diversity and commonality. Examining Irish histories has been one way of achieving these objectives. For example a cross-border, cross-community project examined the meaning of 1916 for Ulster British unionists/loyalists (the Battle of the Somme during World War I) and for Irish nationalists/republicans (the Easter Rising). Out of that discussion, the sacrifice of the Ulster Volunteers *and* the Irish Volunteers at the Somme was revealed comprehensively (McCall, 2011).

Dirk Schubotz (2014) has judged that the future of the Irish peacebuilding process depends on young people. Many cross-border, cross-community projects involved young people in practical, educational, and creative activities. This is important because of the danger that the contemporary peace process – which is older than they are – may be understood by them as a historical event, of little relevance to their lives, rather than as an ongoing, long-term peacebuilding process.

EU Peace programme projects for young people have included the Cultural Pathways project that brought together young people from Protestant East Belfast and 'Southern' Catholic Ballybofey to play music and sport, as well as to discuss issues that interest them and visit each other's home places (McCall, 2011). Another project involved 12 primary schools (500 pupils aged 9 to 12 years) from border regions in Counties Louth, Cavan, Down, Armagh, and Tyrone for local history, local environment, drama, sport, and music activities. The project's finale was an exhibition in the Market Place Theatre, Armagh City, Northern Ireland, of all work undertaken including presentations, drama, songs, and stories (Burke, 2007).

Ramsbotham, Woodhouse, and Miall recognise sport, including football, as 'one important . . . practical entry point for conflict resolvers and a dimension of activity that is transcultural and universal in its appeal' (2011, p. 355). Peace projects with a cross-border, cross-community sports focus have included the Dunfield project, a joint initiative of Linfield Football Club (in Northern Ireland) and Dundalk Football Club (in Ireland) involving 1,000 young people, mostly school pupils. The project organised cross-border, cross-community soccer matches; 'blitz networking' days; 'conflict resolution classes'; and a 'cultural diversity awareness group' (McCall, 2011).

Salmon (2007), meanwhile, maintains that storytelling is an integral element in a conflict transformation enterprise. Many cross-border Peace projects have had storytelling in English, Irish, and Ulster-Scots as their medium in an effort to promote in school pupils an appreciation of cultural diversity through language and dialect. Under the EU Peace programmes storytelling has been the central medium for projects beyond the confines of schools, including carnivals, art in public spaces, documentary filmmaking projects, and projects detailing the life stories of ex-prisoners. The aim has been to challenge strict binary distinctions between 'self' and 'other', 'us' and 'them', 'friends' and 'enemies', 'here' and 'there', 'home' and 'abroad', 'domestic' and 'foreign', 'threat' and 'security', and 'include' and 'exclude' that underpin conflict (McCall and O'Dowd, 2008).

Unlike its predecessors, Peace III (2007–13) did not have a dedicated cross-border cooperation priority commanding a set percentage of the funding. Instead, the programme had two main priorities – 'Reconciling Communities' and 'Contributing to a Shared Society' – through cross-border cooperation was a 'cross-cutting theme'. The Peace III Operational Programme stipulated that cross-border cooperation had been 'mainstreamed' under Peace III.[7] This cross-cutting approach to cross-border cooperation continued with Peace IV (2014–20) where the four main priorities were Shared Education, Children and Young People, Shared Spaces and Services, and Building Positive Relations.[8]

Despite the lack of a dedicated priority, 'cross-cutting', cross-border projects continued to be funded under Peace III with sports, language, and storytelling among their key areas and activities. For example, under the 'Shared Society' priority, Peace III provided €7.8 million for a cross-border sports complex in the 'Clones Erne East' region involving sporting organisations and local authorities from both sides of the (Monaghan/Fermanagh) border and from both communities. A 'Reconciling Communities' cross-community project called 'Yes We Can' developed sporting and cultural links between camogie[9] players and women field hockey players in Northern Ireland. The cross-border element involved project members attending All-Ireland camogie finals at Croke Park, headquarters of the Gaelic Athletic Association.[10] The stories of those on both sides of the border who have been directly affected by the conflict formed the substance of another 'reconciling communities' project called 'Whatever You Say, Say Something' provided by the Healing Through Remembering group. The project's conversation workshops have been led by trained facilitators and are emblematic of a 'bottom-up' approach to conflict transformation (Hamber, 2009).

Peace III also funded literal bridge-building in the form of an iconic €14.5 million foot and cycle 'Peace Bridge' across the River Foyle linking both parts of Derry/Londonderry city and the Donegal hinterland.[11] By July 2009, 75 cross-border projects had received Peace III funding.[12] Under Peace IV, the Cross Border Shared Heritage Communities Programme explored shared heritage between communities in the Mid Ulster District Council and Donegal County Council areas through an exploration of the clans of ancient Ulster.[13] Under the Peace IV 'Children and Young People' priority, the YouthPact project provided youth worker training on peacebuilding for young people.[14] Involving upwards of 10,000 young people aged between 15 and 25, the Youth Network for Peace cross-border project promoted dialogue across a range of hubs, events, conventions, and a youth-led radio station.[15] Meanwhile, the Strive cross-border project focused on engaging marginalised and disadvantaged young people aged between 14 and 24 for the promotion of good relations, personal development, and citizenship.[16]

Challenging stereotypes, discussing history, and recognising diversity and commonality among Irish and Ulster British communities have been important conflict transformation outputs of the Irish borderscape. The emphasis of projects in this borderscape has been on the search for commonality, the acceptance of difference, and the promotion of diversity rather than on attempting to narrow political and cultural differences. Respect for difference is a prerequisite. As Anton Blok observed, 'it is hard for people to survive physically and socially when they are not in some way 'respected'. Violence underwrites cultural reputation [in the absence of respect]' (Blok, 2001, p. ix).

For many involved in cross border, cross-community encounters the Irish borderscape – or Irish/Ulster British borderscape – became a physical and figurative site of communication and contestation wherein meanings could be negotiated through communication rather than challenged by violence. However, sustaining and developing such a physical and figurative borderscape depends on favourable economic and political circumstances on both sides of the Irish border and between Britain and Ireland.

During the years of sustained economic growth in Britain and Ireland that traversed the new millennium, it was not inconceivable to expect the British and Irish governments to assume overall responsibility for sustaining the multitude of local cross-border, cross-community peacebuilding initiatives. This expectation came into sharp relief with the 2004 enlargement of the EU, incorporating eight Central East European states with justifiable claims on the EU's Structural Funds and Community Initiatives. It was given some hope by the Irish government's National Development Plan for 2007–13 which detailed support for infrastructural programmes in Northern Ireland. However, with the global economic crisis beginning in 2008 and the Irish banking crisis culminating in the intervention of the European Central Bank and the International Monetary Fund to rescue the Irish economy in November 2010, it became apparent that fulsome British–Irish intergovernmental support for sustaining cross-border initiatives would not be forthcoming.

In the aftermath of the successful visit of Queen Elizabeth to Ireland in 2012 – the first by a reigning British monarch since partition – the then UK prime minister, David Cameron, enthused that it was a 'game-changer' for British–Irish relations. Perhaps that was the case in terms of public relations and symbolism. Substantively, however, that relationship yielded little in British–Irish intergovernmentalism and cross-border cooperation as both governments pursued their respective economic austerity programmes.

The lack of political dynamism in developing the cross-border institutional infrastructure since its creation in 1998 was obvious to many observers. For instance, in 2012, at the first annual Garret FitzGerald Spring School, the highly respected Irish journalist Olivia O'Leary called for the re-animation of cross-border cooperation at the level of grassroots communities, in the public sector, and in terms of economic and social development in the border region (McCall, 2012).

When in the US, engaged in efforts to generate foreign direct investment and re-establish Ireland's international credentials, the successes of the Irish peace process were recited by Irish ministers. However, back home on Irish soil, ministers paid little attention to substantive peace process concerns, including cross-border cooperation, and appeared content to stray no further than engaging in symbolic acts and visits to the North. Yet long-term peacebuilding and conflict transformation remained an important job of work to do on the island of Ireland, and cross-border cooperation is a central pillar of that endeavour. Therefore, it remained crucial that the Irish cultural borderscape was carefully maintained and developed.

Conclusion

The borderscape concept has been mobilised to capture the cultural and political complexity, contestation, and struggles over inclusion and exclusion in borderlands and border regions. Alternatively, borderscapes can reflect the conflict transformation trinity of contact, communication, and cooperation across a border. EU borderscapes have the potential to become liberating spaces for mobility and intercultural contact, communication, and cooperation that challenge binary distinctions between 'self' and 'other', 'us' and 'them', 'friends' and 'enemies', 'here' and 'there', 'home' and 'abroad', 'domestic' and 'foreign', 'threat' and 'security', and 'include' and 'exclude'. This alternative interpretation of the borderscape concept has been applied to the Irish border region which began to experience conflict transformation in the mid-1990s.

After the Irish republican and Ulster British loyalist ceasefires of 1994, the EU initiated its Peace programmes for Ireland. The cross-border measures of these programmes were innovative policy instruments that developed an Irish cultural borderscape. In that borderscape, cross-border, cross-community contact, communication, and cooperation for long-term peacebuilding and conflict transformation took many forms. Sports, history, and language projects have featured prominently because they are significant cultural resources which provide entry opportunities for cross-border, cross-community contact, communication, and cooperation.

An Irish cultural borderscape in which small-group encounters and interaction have occurred has helped address the political culture of threat and insecurity, downgrade communal antagonism towards 'the Significant Other', and led to the articulation of cultural difference and commonality in a constructive way. Such articulation is embedded in an approach which challenges the reified and homogeneous conceptions of culture associated with Irish and Ulster British communal imaginations, conceptions forged in the fires of violent conflicts. Consequently, this borderscape – which is closely associated with the third (voluntary and community) sector and has involved local 'grassroots' community groups – became reconfigured as one enabling mobility, contact, communication, and cooperation, thus advancing long-term peacebuilding and conflict transformation on the island of Ireland.

For many involved in cross-border, cross-community encounters the Irish cultural borderscape became synonymous with culture as a figurative site of communication and contestation wherein meanings have been continually negotiated through communication rather than challenged by violence. However, sustaining and developing this borderscape depended on the economic and political stars aligning, namely an overarching EU framework, British–Irish intergovernmental cooperation and commitment, favourable economic circumstances, and political cooperation between Irish and Ulster British political parties in Northern Ireland.

After 2008, Ireland's economic collapse and subsequent hair shirt medicine, complemented by the UK's own austerity programme, meant that 'soft capital' enterprises like sustaining the Irish cultural borderscape were in peril. The EU's continued commitment to the Peace programmes alleviated financial vulnerability.[17] However, degrees of complacency by British and Irish governments towards Northern Ireland and the Irish Peace process were increasingly detectable in the years following the Good Friday Agreement. Yet the threat to the Irish cultural borderscape posed by political neglect was as nothing compared to the political thunderbolt delivered by the UK's Brexit referendum on 23 June 2016. It resulted in a majority of 52 to 48 per cent in favour of the United Kingdom of Great Britain and Northern Ireland exiting the EU.

Evidence from the Irish borderscape confirms that a borderscape can be reconfigured as a Peace project. The promotion of cross-border cooperation as peacebuilding, funded by the EU Peace Programmes for Northern Ireland and the border counties of Ireland, yielded an impressive crop of peacebuilding projects that generated contact, communication, and cooperation across the Irish border. Respect for cultural difference and a recognition of similarities were keenly observed by participants in this borderscape. However, the UK's protracted and tortuous withdrawal from the EU and subsequent negotiations on the future EU–UK relationship, between 2016 and 2020, threatened to undermine this peacebuilding enterprise. Brexit rebordering, in the quest to answer the Leave campaign's clarion call – 'take back control' – presented a countervailing force to debordering and cross-border contact, communication, and cooperation on the island of Ireland, with potentially debilitating consequences for conflict transformation and long-term peacebuilding. Instead of conflict transformation, Brexit rebordering appealed to the legacy of Irish border conflict.

Notes

1 www.seupb.eu/sites/default/files/styles/file_entity_browser_thumbnail/public/PEACE%20Content%20Type/The_Impact_of_EU_Funding_in_The_Region.sflb.pdf (accessed 04/04/2020).
2 https://seupb.eu/sites/default/files/styles/PEACEIV/PEACE%20IV%20-%20%20Draft%203.pdf (accessed 04/04/2020).
3 www.interregeurope.eu (accessed 04/04/2020).
4 An east–west, Catholic–Protestant residential divide can be identified within Northern Ireland, with Protestants predominating in the east and Catholics in the west of the region. Moreover, this east–west divide is replicated in many towns and cities in Northern Ireland.
5 www.nicva.org/sites/default/files/d7content/attachments-resources/peace_iv_report_-_final_1_4.pdf and www.osce.org/cio/90147 (both accessed 30/11/2019).
6 In *The European Union and Cross-border Co-operation in Ireland* at www.crossborder.ie/events/Lessons_Colgan.ppt#463,11 (accessed 20/12/2019).
7 https://ec.europa.eu/regional_policy/en/atlas/programmes/2007-2013/crossborder/operational-programme-united-kingdom-ireland-peace-iii (accessed 04/05/2020).
8 www.seupb.eu/sites/default/files/styles/file_entity_browser_thumbnail/public/PEACE%20Content%20Type/PIV_CitizensSummary_English_Version11.pdf (accessed 04/05/2020).
9 Camogie is a women's Gaelic field sport with similarities to hockey.
10 www.irishtimes.com/news/camogie-and-hockey-players-team-up-for-peace-project-1.659007 (accessed 02/04/2020).
11 https://ec.europa.eu/regional_policy/en/newsroom/news/2011/06/commissioner-officially-opens-eu-funded-iconic-peace-bridge-in-northern-ireland (accessed 02/04/2020).
12 SEUPB, 2017. *Peace III Final Report* at 1https://seupb.eu/sites/default/files/styles/Joint_Programme_Docs/PIII_FIR_REVISED_Sept17.PDF (accessed 01/04/2020).
13 www.eurolink-eu.net/european-projects/peace-iv-cross-border-heritage-programme (accessed 01/04/2020).
14 www.cooperationireland.org/youth-pact (accessed 01/04/2020).
15 www.youthaction.org/youth-network-for-peace (accessed 01/04/2020).
16 I am grateful to my PhD student Olivia Brabazon for drawing my attention to these projects.
17 The PEACE PLUS programme runs from 2021 to 2027. See www.seupb.eu/peaceplus (accessed 05/05/2020).

4 Rebordering

Introduction

Rebordering denotes the reintroduction of customs posts, inspection points, and a border security regime to reinforce border infrastructure and protect border control personnel. Brexit – the withdrawal of the UK from the EU – proposed major constitutional upheaval for the UK, with serious economic and political implications for the island of Ireland and for the manifestation of the Irish border. Opposition to immigration and the freedom of movement of EU workers to Britain was a major reason for the success of the Leave campaign in the 2016 Brexit referendum. Consequently, a central focus of Brexit was the perceived need for rebordering, that is the strengthening of Britain's border as a security barrier to prevent the movement of 'unwanted outsiders' to Britain and 'take back control'.

On the face of it, Brexit presented three rebordering possibilities: reborder the UK (including the Irish border), reborder Britain (excluding the Irish border), or reborder the 'British Isles' (including the island of Ireland). In reality, there were only two possibilities: no Irish government was ever going to voluntarily compromise the hard-won sovereignty of the state and risk Ireland's membership of the EU into the bargain by acquiescing to the extension of Brexit rebordering that enveloped the whole of the island of Ireland. Moreover, it would not be prepared to expose a small state – Ireland – to the vagaries of an asymmetrical relationship with a large and powerful neighbour which was devoted to a 'Global Britain' project.

From the perspective of Ireland, membership of the EC/EU had helped to calibrate the British–Irish relationship and protect Ireland's interests. Nevertheless, Brexit rebordering had the potential to turn the tide against decades of debordering *on* the island of Ireland that was delivered by Europeanisation, the North–South provisions of the 1998 Good Friday Agreement, and a wealth of EU-funded cross-border cooperation initiatives.

From an open Irish border vantage point, this chapter explores the two Brexit rebordering options: reborder the island of Ireland and reborder Britain.

From debordering to rebordering

The debordering impulse of the 1990s was challenged by twenty-first-century dramatisations – the downing of the Twin Towers in New York by Islamic jihadists in 2001 and the Mediterranean migration/refugee crisis peaking in 2015 – that gave rise to an increased perception of risks and threats from international terrorism and contested migration. The EU response was to attempt to reinforce the EU as a 'gated community'. It deployed sophisticated selection mechanisms which determine the entry of individuals with the aim of protecting European citizens from multifarious threats emanating from beyond the gates (van Houtum and Pijpers, 2007, p. 303). The political aim has been to protect the EU from far-right populists and left-wing statist ideologues within who have sought the disintegration of the EU. As a consequence, EU cross-border cooperation shifted from being a debordering dynamic towards a rebordering one through the increased emphasis on border securitisation across the EU's external frontier (Andreas, 2003; Walters, 2006; McCall, 2014). Thus, while the EU has 'sought to valorize transnational spaces through cross-border and inter-regional co-operation programmes' (Keating, 2010, p. 30), its twenty-first-century emphasis on 'security' has involved building an EU external frontier to protect EU citizens from perceived external threats and the EU itself from internal ones.

Borders remain the principal foci for securitising mobility (Amoore, 2006). Indeed, some EU member states, including Austria and Hungary, attempted to take rebordering into their own hands and secure their state borders in the face of the Mediterranean migration/refugee crisis. Even the pre-eminent symbol of European debordering, the Øresund Bridge connecting Denmark and Sweden, was affected by the rebordering thrust spurred by the migration/refugee crisis when identity checks on commuters crossing the border from Denmark were introduced by Sweden in 2016.[1] These individual member state initiatives may be understood as performances in temporarily re-asserting the authority of the state (Peoples and Vaughan-Williams, 2015, p. 175). They confirm that debordering and rebordering are competing and overlapping processes in the twenty-first-century EU (Amilhat Szary and Giraut, 2015, p. 4).

In the context of Britain and Ireland, Brexit means rebordering. The freedom of movement of labour across EU borders captured a substantial segment of the British/English national imagination because it was held to be responsible for breaching the imagined parameters that give meaning to Britain/England, Britishness/Englishness, and the contemporary 'British/English way of life'. Objection to freedom of movement reflected the ambivalent attitude of the British/English to the relationship between Britain/England and Europe since the end of World War II (Bogdanor, 2020).

The Brexit referendum campaign was informed by concerns, prejudices, fears, and insecurities relating to the mobility of EU workers, as well as a media spotlight on contested migration, in the contexts of a prolonged period of economic austerity and the EU's Mediterranean migration/refugee crisis (Carl, 2018). The emphasis on bordering and security requires the installation of a hard security border regime in order to prevent the movement of these 'unwanted outsiders' to Britain, including those coming from within the EU and thus remove an 'existential threat' to British/English identity (Buzan, 1993).

Michael Keating identified three groups under the Brexit umbrella: the 'Europeans', who prioritised access to the European Single Market without the political consequences; the 'Little Englanders', who opposed EU membership or affiliation; and the 'Globalists', who resented EU regulation and believed that the UK could become a global economic superpower again in its own right (Keating, 2016). However, objection to the EU's freedom of movement of labour principle was a primary motivating factor uniting Brexiters of all stripes.

The threat from contested migration made regular headlines in the English media, particularly in the right-wing tabloid press. Calais, Sangatte, and 'the Jungle' were portrayed as sites of perennial threat for Britain/England and 'the British/English way of life'.[2] Chaotic scenes of contested migrants attempting mass crossings of the English Channel via the Channel Tunnel provided the necessary drama for prioritising the issue in British politics. Reacting to this drama in July 2015, the then UK prime minister, David Cameron, intensified it further when he proclaimed that 'you have got *a swarm* of people coming across the Mediterranean, seeking a better life, wanting to come to Britain because Britain has got jobs, it's got a growing economy, it's an incredible place to live' (author's emphasis). Such a 'speech act' has been identified as an important component of a securitisation process that emphasises rebordering (Waever, 1995): 'the swarm' is the threat; hard security borders are the answer to that threat. The slow burn of the post-2004 arrival of 'legitimate' mobile workers from Central Eastern Europe became the prejudicial bedrock of this securitisation process. According to Cameron, 'the bigger issue today is migration from within the EU. Numbers that have increased faster than we in this country wanted . . . at a level that was too much for our communities, for our labour markets'.[3]

Brexit was a direct consequence of the strengthening of Eurosceptic and Europhobe lobbies within the British Conservative Party and beyond it. For Roger Liddle, the Brexit campaign was 'the remorseless logic of Conservative division on the European question' (2015, p. 5). With Prime Minister Cameron leading a Conservative majority British government after May 2015, Brexit became firmly placed on the UK political agenda. The EU freedom of movement of labour principle was a key focal point (O'Ceallaigh and Gillespie, 2015, p. 223).

In the UK, the state security rebordering process was already well advanced, symbolised by large signs declaring 'UK Border' in the international arrival halls of UK airports. The UK border security regime already was a sophisticated response to perceived threats emanating from *Outre-Mer* and had been largely focused on 'border portals' and 'choke points' – airports, seaports, and the Channel Tunnel. The Channel Tunnel is a particular point of interest for those concerned with rebordering Britain to halt contested immigration. Unlike a land border, the Channel Tunnel is a singular port of entry or 'choke point' through which all vehicles, goods, and people have to pass and, as such, should present a relatively straightforward site for the exercise of a security regime (Anderson and Bort, 2001, p. 184). A greater challenge is patrolling the 10,500 miles of maritime borders around UK and the multiple ports of entry, including 120 commercial ports.[4] The British border security regime also involved activities in cyberspace wherein the biometric passport – 'the border in the pocket' – and the smartphone with GPS superseded many, but not all, of the traditional functions of the human border guard (Häkli, 2015, p. 93).

Despite this extensive border security regime, Brexiters remained unimpressed by 'the border in the pocket'. They were impervious to the fact that Britain's border zone extended territorially to the European continent, with British border guards, replete with a formidable armoury of electronic border control paraphernalia – information databases, x-ray machines, electronic fingerprinters, body scanners, heat-seeking cameras, robots, and probes – stationed in Boulogne, Brussels, Calais, Coquelles, Dunkerque, Frethun, Lille, and Paris. They were unimpressed by the creation of an eclectic security border zone around Britain involving border intelligence agents such as airline liaison officers who advise foreign law enforcement agencies on the potential cross-border movement of people deemed to be 'illegitimate' or 'undesirable' travellers (Vaughan-Williams, 2009). And as far as British intelligence agencies are concerned, it would be antithetical for them to publicise their activities in the governance of border control.

Conversely, Brexiters enjoyed a high profile in British politics and the media, their cause helped by the Mediterranean migration/refugee crisis, by arresting television images of contested migrants attempting to cross the English Channel, and by the *Polski Smak* (Polish Flavour) of the rapidly changing twenty-first-century British high street. In other words, efforts to create an eclectic border zone around Britain – through offshore bordering practices and adventures in cybersecurity – did not neutralise the perceived threat posed by 'unwanted outsiders', including legitimate mobile EU workers, to the contemporary 'British/English way of life'.

Rebordering the Irish border

The 'take back control' mantra of Brexit demanded the creation of clear, hard territorial security borders that proved to be impenetrable for 'unwanted outsiders'. The EU also required, at a minimum, a border inspection and customs regime to protect its Single Market and operationalise its Customs Union because they are core elements of the EU. The barely perceptible Irish border is the only land border that the UK shares with another member state, Ireland.[5] It proved to be a major stumbling block for Brexiters in their trek to the 'sunlit uplands of global Britain' freed from the shackles of the EU.[6]

One British politician appeared to recognise the Irish border challenge from the outset. Supporting 'Remain' in the Brexit referendum, then British home secretary (later prime minister) Theresa May claimed that 'it is inconceivable that a vote for Brexit would not have a negative impact on the North South [Irish] Border, bringing cost and disruption to trade and to people's lives'.[7] After becoming prime minister, May determined that 'of course Northern Ireland will have a border with the Republic of Ireland, which will remain a member of the European Union'.[8]

Post-Brexit, Ireland would continue as an EU member state and abide by its 'four freedoms': the free movement of goods, capital, services, and people. From a traditional sovereign state perspective, therefore, the Irish border would be a focus for the British government's effort to 'take back control' and for the EU to ensure the integrity of the EU Customs Union and its Single Market. However, rebordering the Irish border was problematic for logistical, economic, and political reasons.

Logistical problems

Logistical problems stemmed from the fact that the Irish border runs for 499 kilometres through towns, townlands, mountains, loughs, bogs, fields, farms, and some homes. Officially, it has 208 crossing points. The island of Ireland has the densest cross-border road network in Europe. It has nearly twice as many cross-border roads as those crossing the EU's entire eastern external frontier. In comparison, a mere 21 roads cross the border between England and Scotland.[9] Moreover, the Irish border and road interaction are anarchic. The border runs down the middle of 11 roads, including a section of the M1 Dublin–Newry motorway.[10] Key arterial roads can cross the border more than once. For example, the direct route from Cavan Town (County Cavan, Ireland) to Dungannon (County Tyrone, Northern Ireland) through the Drummully Salient crosses the border no less than five times.

The leading Brexiter MP Jacob Rees-Mogg considered rebordering the Irish border when he pronounced that 'there would be our ability, as we had during the Troubles, to have people inspected'.[11] Prior to the Single Market coming into effect in 1993, there were 15 customs and agri-food inspection points on key cross-border arterial routes. A similar number of customs and agri-food inspection points would be required in the event of post-Brexit rebordering. Moreover, rebordering would also require the closure and securement (by bollards or explosives) of almost 200 minor cross-border roads that were re-opened during the debordering era.

Should 'Troubles-era arrangements' have re-visited the Irish border, who or what would have been doing the inspecting? Technology could be applied to the management of Irish border security. Devices such as motion sensors, registration plate recognition scanners, and infra-red and surveillance cameras, as well as migration databases, could be deployed in that management. The Legatum Institute – the influential Brexit 'think tank' in London – even proposed the 'persistent surveillance of the border region' by unmanned aerial vehicles (drones) after Brexit[12] (Singham et al., 2017, p. 28). However, to recommend that technology would have rendered a post-Brexit Irish border 'invisible' was rejected out of hand by border technology experts (Taylor, 2017).

Without the human border guards, sensors, scanners, cameras, and databases serve as recording and counting devices of border crossings (Broeders, 2011, pp. 40–1). Such components of artificial intelligence provide the reckoning of border crossings, but it is the human border guard who provides the judgement on such crossings on which decisions rests (Cantwell Smith, 2019). Additionally, in the case of the meandering Irish border, technological infrastructure on cross-border roads would have been no less vulnerable to destruction than 'Welcome to Northern Ireland' signs unless it was protected by human border patrols. Tellingly, a 2018 survey conducted in the Central Border Region found that a majority of the 600 respondents claimed that they would not accept border control technology even if it was unmanned and located away from the border (Hayward, 2018). In any case, Karine Côté-Boucher (2016, 2020) has found that there is a distinct preference among border guards for 'low tech' – the gun and other weaponry – as effective border control tools, over the 'high tech'.

At the outset of the EU–UK Brexit negotiations the British government's position paper *Northern Ireland and Ireland* (Department for Exiting the European Union and Northern Ireland Office, 2017) stated that it wanted the Irish border to remain 'as seamless and frictionless as possible'. If this statement reflected a desire to maintain the *status quo*, namely an open border with the free flow of goods and people across it, then there was an obvious clash with the British government's greater desire: leave the EU (including the Single Market and Customs Union), escape the purview of the European Court of Justice, 'take back control' of it borders, and end the free movement of people. Since Brexit was inspired by the desire to curb freedom of movement of labour from the European continent, it did not seem plausible that the British government could entertain the continuation of an open Irish border. Nigel Lawson, the former UK chancellor of the exchequer and chairman of the Vote Leave campaign, conceded that 'there would have to be border controls'. When he was parliamentary under secretary of state at the Ministry of Justice,[13] Dominic Raab confirmed that '[i]f you're worried about border controls and security . . . you couldn't leave a back door without some kind, either of checks there with any country or assurances in relation to the checks that they're conducting, obviously'.[14]

Political problems

Rebordering the Irish border would also have reignited political problems relating to a history of violent border conflict on the island. The Irish border was the subject of agitation and violence from its consolidation in 1925 until the beginning of the debordering process in the early 1990s. Violence became an endemic feature of the Irish border region during the Troubles (Patterson, 2013). However, the border security regime remained partial spatially because the British government recognised that a continuous securitised border along its 499-kilometre length would play into the hands of anti-partitionist Irish politicians and republican insurgents. In other words, the partiality of border security was due to the fact that there was 'no political will at Westminster' for its imposition because of the concern that such a move would further stir political Irish nationalism and militant Irish republicanism (Rose, 1983, p. 3).

With 'no political will at Westminster' to secure the Irish border during the Northern Ireland 'Troubles', such an undertaking after Brexit would have been interpreted as a demonstration of wanton political neglect. All the more so because debordering – through the removal of security checkpoints and customs posts, as well as the promotion of North–South (Belfast–Dublin) and cross-border cooperation – has been an important element in

British–Irish peacebuilding. The implications of rebordering for the Irish cultural borderscape, and the peacebuilding process generally, were ominous, not least because rebordering disrupts mobility, contact, communication, and cooperation across the border (McCall, 2018; Murphy, 2018; Wilson, 2019).

Yet, for Brexit ideologues led by British cabinet ministers Dominic Raab, Michael Gove, and Jacob Rees-Mogg, Brexit was akin to the marvellous medicine brewed by young George Kranky in Roald Dahl's children's classic *George's Marvellous Medicine*. It had

> a brutal and bewitching smell, spicy and staggering, fierce and frenzied full of wizardry and magic. Whenever he got a whiff of it up his nose firecrackers went off in his skull and electric prickles ran down the backs of his legs. It was wonderful to stand there stirring this amazing mixture and to watch it smoking blue and bubbling and frothing and foaming as though it were alive.
>
> (Dahl, 2016, p. 33)

The years of Brexit 'bubbling, frothing and foaming' after the Brexit referendum created alarm and trepidation among Irish borderlanders and Irish people across the island of Ireland, as well as those abroad. Soothing words from the Breixters at Westminister that there would be 'no hard border' on the island of Ireland cut little ice when the possibility of a 'no deal' Brexit could result in rebordering the Irish border.

In *Candide* by Voltaire, the protagonist complains that 'Pangloss most cruelly deceived me when he said that everything in the world is for the best' (1991, p. 18). Irish people were not deceived by the 'no hard border' soft soaping of Panglossian British Conservative politicians. From an Irish perspective, their Brexit 'bubbling, frothing and foaming' confirmed that these gentlemen could not be employed to mind mice at the crossroads never mind be cognisant of, or care about, Irish interests while negotiating through the Brexit maze.

Upon becoming British prime minister on 23 July 2019, Boris Johnson found that Ireland and the Irish border were major obstacles in his push to reach the 'sunlit uplands' of post-Brexit Britain. A century earlier, his lodestar, Winston Churchill, as secretary of state for the colonies, voiced frustration at the way in which Ireland had impinged on 'British life and politics':

> Great Empires have been overturned. The whole map of Europe has been changed. The position of countries has been violently altered. The modes of thought of men, the whole outlook on affairs, the grouping of parties, all have encountered violent and tremendous changes in the

> deluge of the world, but as the deluge subsides and the waters fall short we see the dreary steeples of Fermanagh and Tyrone emerging once again. The integrity of their quarrel is one of the few institutions that has been unaltered in the cataclysm which has swept the world. That says a lot for the persistency with which Irish men on the one side or the other are able to pursue their controversies. It says a great deal for the power which Ireland has, both Nationalist and Orange, to lay their hands upon the vital strings of British life and politics, and to hold, dominate, and convulse, year after year, generation after generation, the politics of this powerful country.
>
> (16 February 1922)[15]

One hundred years later would Irish people, in Fermanagh and Tyrone and beyond, once again frustrate British ambitions and the politics of that powerful country? Rebordering along the Irish border could be attempted: establish customs, agri-food inspection, and immigration checkpoints on Irish cross-border arterial routes; close hundreds of secondary cross-border roads; and recruit border security personnel to support vulnerable customs and inspection officials and infrastructure in isolated terrain. Politically, however, the deleterious consequences of such rebordering for cross-border contact, communication and cooperation, and, therefore, peacebuilding, were clear, not to mention the risk of a return to the politically motivated agitation and violence of the past.

In the context of two decades of painstaking peacebuilding work the post-referendum years of Brexit 'bubbling, frothing and foaming' had already damaged the Irish cultural borderscape and the respect that it nurtured for British and Irish identities. Binary distinctions between Remain and Leave (the EU), 'self' and 'other', 'us' and 'them', 'friends' and 'enemies', 'here' and 'there', 'home' and 'abroad', 'domestic' and 'foreign', 'threat' and 'security', and 'include' and 'exclude' began to re-ossify as the effort by the British government to withdraw the UK from the EU and recast the UK–EU relationship continued on an elongated and tortuous path. This was precisely the opposite direction of travel from the one that had been pursued in the Irish cultural borderscape wherein a genuine effort was made to explore, accommodate, and celebrate commonalities and differences.

Economic problems

An unforeseen bonus of two decades of debordering was the development of the all-island economy, particularly in the agri-food sector.[16] Complex cross-border supply chains developed during the debordering era. In the milk sector, for example, 600 million litres of milk produced in Northern Ireland per annum crossed the border to be processed in Ireland. The 120 million litres sold as liquid milk in Ireland accounted for 25 per cent of the milk supply south of the border. The imposition of tariffs and Single Market regulations would have threatened to sever this supply and decimate the livelihoods of northern dairy farmers. Similarly, live-animal cross-border movement, including half a million pigs per annum, was also threatened should post-Brexit Northern Ireland have deviated from EU rules on animal safety, animal health and welfare, disease control, and traceability (Connelly, 2017).

It was not as if the British government was blissfully unaware of the highly integrated cross-border supply chains and the potential economic problems for the island of Ireland that would have been encountered as a result of 'no deal' Brexit rebordering on the island of Ireland. Its own report *Operation Yellowhammer: HMG Reasonable Worst Case Planning Assumptions* (2 August 2019), which was stamped 'OFFICIAL SENSITIVE', presented an arresting 'no deal' vista of economic disruption and collapse, job losses and subsequent protests, and direct action in the Irish borderscape. The report also anticipated a 'growth of the illegitimate economy' otherwise known as 'smuggling'.

The EU Customs Union rendered Irish border customs checkpoints redundant because import duties were no longer to be collected. However, excise duties on fuel, alcohol, and tobacco remained. Smuggling thus became a highly profitable niche activity that was the preserve of well-organised cross-border criminal gangs. It was entirely possible that their activities would have been 'turbo-charged' by a Brexit that resulted in import/export duties and North–South regulatory divergence.[17] As Peter Neumann declares,

> it is the golden law of smuggling. If you have two jurisdictions and you have a desirable product that is hard to get hold of on one side of the border and easier to get hold of on the other side of the border, somebody will turn up and turn that into a profit.[18]

The organised and experienced were the most likely candidates to turn up.

In this scenario, mobile security patrols along the unwieldy 499 kilometres of the Irish border would have been almost irresistible, not least to help protect vulnerable customs officials and agri-food inspectors working in isolated border terrain. Such an introduction would have been made more likely by the fact that the peace process and the openness of the border led to the closure of 40 per cent of police stations on either side of the border.[19] In these circumstances new security personnel would have been required from outside and would have been unfamiliar with the area, unknown to borderlanders, and characterised by them as 'nameless, faceless strangers'.

Alienation and antagonism would have seeped back into the borderlands as a result.

Chiefs of police on both sides of the border were acutely aware of potential 'no deal' policing challenges along the border.[20] These challenges were posed not only by the possible return of alienation, antagonism, and the likely strengthening of politically motivated 'dissident' Irish republicans but also by well-organised, cross-border smugglers motivated by profit.

Reborder Britain

During the negotiations on the UK's exit from the EU, alternatives to rebordering on the island of Ireland were proposed. Phase 1 negotiations entertained the option of ports and airports in Britain and Northern Ireland becoming the foci for customs and border inspections. Such an approach meant that Northern Ireland would remain aligned to the EU Customs Union and Single Market to the effect that such inspections would not be required on the Irish border but would be established at an 'Irish Sea Border', that is at ports in Britain and on the island of Ireland. For its part, the British government appeared to be committed to a no-tariff deal for Northern Irish goods entering Britain. This scenario was intimated in the linguistic contortions of the 'Joint Report from the Negotiators of the European Union and the United Kingdom Government on Progress During Phase 1 of Negotiations under Article 50 TEU on the United Kingdom's Orderly Withdrawal from the European Union' (European Commission, 8 December 2017, para. 49 and 50).

Rebordering Britain rather than the UK had three distinct advantages: first, it would honour a cross-border, cross-community democratic wish articulated in the oft-repeated refrain in the political domain, namely 'no one wants to see a hard border' on the island of Ireland;[21] second, it would be logistically easier and economically less costly to establish and manage; and, third, it would avoid the risk of a return to the political agitation and violence associated with a hard Irish border. As Kapka Kassabova contends, 'an actively policed [territorial] border is always aggressive: it is where power suddenly acquires a body, if not a human face, and an ideology' (2017, p. xvi). In the case of the Irish border, bordering would require bodies with (concealed) human faces which would re-dramatise the conflicting Ulster British and Irish nationalist ideologies that two decades of debordering had helped to calm.

Securing the borders of Britain – rather than those of the UK – has historical precedent. During World War II, after the fall of France in 1940, Irish travellers were required to carry passports or limited travel documents for 'war-work' to gain entry to Britain. A full return to freedom of movement in a 'common travel area' did not happen until 1952 (Meehan, 2000, p. 26). Bordering Britain became a reality again for some under the 1974 Prevention of Terrorism (Temporary Provisions) Act in response to the Irish Republican Army bombing of two public houses in Birmingham. The act gave the British home secretary the power to prevent individuals moving from Northern Ireland to Britain and to deport individuals from Britain to Northern Ireland:

> If the Secretary of State is satisfied that-
>
> a) any person (whether in Great Britain or elsewhere) is concerned in the commission, preparation or instigation of acts of terrorism, or
> b) any person is attempting or may attempt to enter Great Britain with a view to being concerned in the commission, preparation or instigation of acts of terrorism,
>
> the Secretary of State may make an order against that person prohibiting him from being in, or entering, Great Britain.[22]

Passengers at the 'Belfast Gate' of Britain's airports were accustomed to the intrusion of border portal control paraphernalia long before the experience became widespread after the drama of the 11 September 2001 Islamic jihadist attacks on the US. Such bordering between Great Britain and Northern Ireland is problematic for the idea of a UK border that is coterminous with the UK state. For Richard Rose, Britain is the *de facto* state, and its borders are 'fuzzy' (1983, pp. 31–2). The logic of Brexit is that the UK border would retreat to Britain, and perhaps to England, in the Brexiter quest to render it, clear, secure, and impenetrable to 'unwanted outsiders'.

Elizabeth Meehan maintained that 'Great Britain being an island is still crucial to the outlooks of governments on the maintenance of frontier controls' (2000, p. 60). British public opinion reflects the position of British governments on Britain's border. In an ICM opinion poll published in the *Guardian* newspaper on 21 August 2001, the question posed to a sample of Britons in Britain was 'Do you think Northern Ireland should be part of the UK?' Twenty-six per cent responded that it should remain part of the UK, 41 per cent that it should be joined with Ireland, and 33 per cent responded 'don't know'.

British opinion on Northern Ireland as a member of the UK remained unenthusiastic two decades later. In 2018, a YouGov/LBC survey found that a majority of those surveyed prioritised Britain leaving the EU (36 per cent) over maintaining the union between Northern Ireland and the rest of the UK

(29 per cent).[23] In 2019, a Lord Ashcroft Poll, with a sample of 1558 adults in England, found that 35 per cent thought that Northern Ireland should remain part of the UK while 13 per cent said that it should not. However, while 10 per cent opted for 'don't know' in the poll, 43 per cent didn't care: "I don't have a view – it's for the people of NI [Northern Ireland] to decide'.[24] Also in 2019, a YouGov poll found that 43 per cent of Britons in Britain 'don't have a strong view' on what should happen to Northern Ireland while 15 per cent thought it should be joined with 'the rest of Ireland'. That poll's findings indicated that the preferred outcome on Brexit matters much more to Britons than Northern Ireland staying in the UK: 58 per cent opted for the former and only 18 per cent for the latter.[25]

Such polls make stark and unwelcome reading for Ulster British unionists in Northern Ireland. Responding to the findings of the YouGov/LBC survey, Democratic Unionist Party (DUP) MP Sir Jeffery Donaldson invoked the Good Friday Agreement (which the DUP opposed) in an attempt to support the Ulster British unionist position: 'The Good Friday Agreement states very clearly that the principle of consent means that it's for the people of Northern Ireland alone to decide whether we remain part of the United Kingdom'.[26] By way of contrast, in a 2019 RED C exit poll for Raidió Teilifís Éireann (RTÉ) and TG4, 65 per cent of those polled in Ireland (the state) indicated they would vote for a 'united Ireland' if a referendum was held 'tomorrow', 19 per cent would vote against such a proposal, and 15 per cent opted for 'don't know' or refused to answer the question.[27]

After entering into a 'confidence and supply' supportive arrangement with the post-2017 general election minority Conservative British government, with Theresa May as prime minister, it appeared that the DUP's opposition to bordering Britain was shorn up by that British government. Its Department for Exiting the European Union rejected the idea of locating Brexit customs controls at ports and airports, stating that 'we cannot create a Border between Northern Ireland and Great Britain' (Staunton, 2017). However, as the negotiations continued and the draft Withdrawal Treaty was published, it became clear that a bordering Britain alternative was included in the form of 'the backstop'.

Backstop

'The backstop' became the major bone of contention in the *Draft Agreement on the Withdrawal of the United Kingdom of Great Britain and Northern Ireland from the European Union and the European Atomic Energy Community* (European Commission, 2018).[28] 'The backstop' was contained in the Draft Agreement's Protocol on Ireland/Northern Ireland. The protocol decreed that, in the event of the failure to agree to a comprehensive EU/UK trade agreement after a transition period or find other (technology-based) solutions for maintaining an open Irish border, the backstop would come into effect. It would keep the whole of the UK in a single customs territory with the EU. Additionally, Northern Ireland would remain in some parts of the Single Market to ensure the preservation of an open Irish border without inspection points.

The Draft Agreement was rejected three times by MPs in the British House of Commons.[29] With Leave-inclined Conservative MPs voting en masse against the agreement, it is a point of conjecture whether the main reason for this repeated rejection was the backstop's divergent regulatory regime for Northern Ireland from the rest of the UK or the proposed UK–EU common customs territory that the UK could not exit unilaterally. Polls indicating a lukewarm British/English attitude to Northern Ireland's place in the UK indicates that the latter inspired Conservative rejectionists.

What the Draft Agreement did do was help bring a premature end the premiership of Theresa May. Subsequently, the two candidates for the prime minister vacancy, Boris Johnson and Jeremy Hunt, both declared that they would not accept any backstop in future negotiations with the EU and that a 'no deal' Brexit would be preferable to the backstop.[30] However, the Groucho Marx quip 'Those are my principles, and if you don't like them . . . well I have others' applied to the victorious candidate, Boris Johnson, with his proven track record of being less than resolute on points of principle.

The DUP was implacably opposed to the backstop interpreting it as a vehicle to create 'a border down the Irish Sea' and separate Northern Ireland from the rest of the UK. Yet the backstop could have helped to achieve many of the priorities stipulated by DUP leader Arlene Foster as first minister of Northern Ireland in a letter (co-signed by Deputy First Minister Martin McGuinness) to Prime Minister Theresa May, first and foremost that 'the [Irish] border will not become an impediment to the movement of people, goods, and services'. They also stressed the need to retain the ease of trading relationships with EU member states, the protection of the agri-food sector, and the requirement that the border does not incentivise 'those who would wish to undermine the peace process'.[31]

The backstop was essentially a compromise by the EU and the British government designed to accommodate the desires expressed in the Foster/McGuinness letter. The EU compromised on its Single Market by permitting Northern Ireland to remain in parts of it pertaining to the border and the all-island economy in the event of the backstop coming into effect. The British government compromised on the sovereignty of the UK by agreeing to special arrangements for Northern Ireland with respect to the remit of the Single Market and by agreeing to remain in an EU–UK customs territory (Hayward, 2019a). However, the political clout of Brexiters determined that *compromise* was a dirty word in the House of Commons.

During a 2018 Brexit debate, the DUP MP Ian Paisley Jr roared, 'No Surrender to the EU', across the floor of the House of Commons, recalling the uncompromising ranting of his father during the Troubles.[32] In her last speech before stepping down as prime minister, Theresa May bemoaned the absolutionism of Brexiters, saying, 'An inability to combine principles with pragmatism and make a compromise when required seems to have driven our whole political discourse down the wrong path'.[33]

Frontstop

The Revised Withdrawal Agreement, containing the Revised Protocol on Ireland/Northern Ireland, was negotiated by Boris Johnson's government and released on 17 October 2019. It confirmed that the British government reflected British popular opinion by caring not a fig for the membership of Northern Ireland as a constituent part of the UK. Rather, the overriding priority was to disentangle Britain from the tentacles of EU law and governance. The desire for divergence between Britain and the EU trumped the one for maintaining the status of Northern Ireland as an integral part of the UK.

The Revised Protocol shifted the focus of rebordering decisively from the Irish border to one between the island of Ireland and Britain, and the reinforcement of an 'Irish Sea border'. It revealed that Northern Ireland would follow EU rules and regulations on customs and goods while Britain would not. Unlike the backstop, the frontstop is assumed to be permanent. However, Northern Ireland Members of the Legislative Assembly (MLAs) would have the opportunity to vote to opt out of protocol arrangements every four years (McGarry and O'Leary, 2019).

Northern Ireland would remain a part of the UK customs territory – with Northern Ireland nominally included in future UK trade deals – yet, in effect, it would follow the EU's customs code. EU Value-Added Tax rules would apply to Northern Ireland, and it would follow EU rules and regulations for trade (Hayward, 2019b). This arrangement could be interpreted as 'the best of both worlds' for Northern Ireland: non-tariff access to both EU and British markets. However, Katy Hayward cautioned that its practical outworking could leave Northern Ireland 'between a rock and a hard place'. The establishment of an 'Irish Sea Border' would likely negatively impact the free movement of goods within the UK single market. With Northern Ireland being, in effect, a part of the EU Customs Union, declarations would be required on goods moving from Northern Ireland to Britain with disruptive consequences for Northern Ireland businesses operating on a west–east – Northern Ireland to Britain – basis. Goods moving east–west – from Britain to Northern Ireland – would require customs declarations and animal products moving in that direction would be liable to inspection at

Northern Ireland airports and mainly at its seaports of Belfast, Larne, Foyle, and Warrenpoint (Connelly, 2020b; Hayward, 2020a).

Full stop?

There was a further sting in the Brexit tail for the island of Ireland with the publication of the *United Kingdom Internal Market Bill* in September 2020. Clauses 42 through 45 of the bill threatened to override parts of the Revised Withdrawal Agreement and the Protocol on Ireland/Northern Ireland and break international law in the process. The bill invested the British secretary of state for Northern Ireland with the power to 'modify or disapply' the protocol's requirement for export declarations relating to goods transported between Northern Ireland and Great Britain. It also gave the secretary of state the power to interpret Article 10 of the protocol on state aid.

The protocol decreed that EU state aid rules applied to Northern Ireland. Moreover, if companies based in Britain have a footprint in Northern Ireland, they could also be liable to follow EU state aid rules (Connelly, 2020a; Hayward, 2020b). The acerbic political journalist and Westminster insider Andrew Rawnsley (2020) speculated that state aid rules affecting businesses in Britain, rather than the 'Irish Sea Border', was what rankled with Boris Johnson and Dominic Cummings, the prime minister's special adviser and Rasputin-in-chief. Cummings's masterplan for prolonged Conservative Party electoral success involved state aid for high-tech business ventures, especially in the north of England where the Labour Party dominated until the Conservative Party's win in the 2019 general election. Thus, English concerns appeared to override Irish interests. However, the abrupt departure of Cummings from the prime minister's 10 Downing Street team in November 2020, together with the election of Joe Biden[34] as president of the US that same month, placed a question mark against the offending articles. Indeed, they were dropped from the *United Kingdom Internal Market Bill* the following month during the final stages of negotiations on the future EU–UK relationship.[35]

Irish Sea Border

Negotiations on the EU–UK future divorced relationship resulted in the Draft EU–UK Trade and Cooperation Agreement which was reached on Christmas Eve 2020.[36] The Draft Agreement facilitated the tariff-free and quota-free movement of goods between the EU and the UK. However, non-tariff barriers between the EU and the UK still applied. On services, there was some provision for market access but with many exceptions. On the free movement of people, there would be visa-free travel for holidaymakers for up to 90 days. The freedom of movement for workers would, of course, come to an end. Indeed, the EU freedom of movement across goods, capital, services, and people ended for Great Britain on 31 December 2020 (Phinnemore, 2020). Moreover, years and years and years of argument and rankle on the outworkings, accusations of 'bad faith', and disputes regarding both the Withdrawal Agreement and the Trade Agreement in the EU–UK Partnership Council, committees, and beyond could be anticipated.

At the end of the negotiations, the Withdrawal Agreement's Protocol on Ireland/Northern Ireland was upheld. It provided for Northern Ireland remaining, *de facto*, in the EU Single Market and EU Customs Union. From 1 January 2021, border customs and inspection points for goods entering the island of Ireland were operationalised, especially at seaports, including the Northern Ireland seaports of Belfast, Larne, Foyle, and Warrenpoint. Customs and inspection points located there and elsewhere on the island of Ireland effectively constituted the 'Irish Sea Border'. Ostensibly, therefore, the 'Irish Sea Border' meant that the Irish border on the island of Ireland would remain in a debordering frame.[37]

Conclusion

During the Northern Ireland 'Troubles', the political risks of a continuous and 'seamless' (in the security barrier sense) Irish border were recognised by the British government. That border had undergone a 20-year reconfiguration – driven by Europeanisation, the North–South provisions of the Good Friday Agreement, and an avalanche of EU-funded cross-border cooperation initiatives – that rendered it open and free-flowing for unhindered mobility, contact, communication, cooperation, and trade.

The Brexit Leave campaign reverberated with the mantra 'take back control'. Rebordering was a principal mechanism for asserting such control. In the context of the Irish border, Brexit presented the possibility of rebordering on the island of Ireland. It would have necessitated hundreds of secondary cross-border road closures, border checkpoints on main arterial routes, and mobile border security patrols. The prospect of such an eventuality vividly re-dramatised the power dynamic and conflict between Ulster British unionist and Irish nationalist ideologies which had been calmed by two decades of debordering. However, the economic cost, logistical difficulties, and political risks in doing so meant another rebordering option be explored.

The alternative option was to reborder Britain. The border of Britain is the UK border in the British national imagination. The border of Britain is an imagined border that is disseminated by the British media, endorsed by the political establishment, and reflected in the British public attitudes. There are historical precedents for such bordering, notably during and after World

War II. However, this option was problematic for Ulster British unionists in Northern Ireland and, potentially, for the Irish peace process if perceptions of their abandonment took hold. Nevertheless, rebordering Britain would be relatively simple to establish and would cause the least disruption given the fact that border portals – seaports and airports – are long-established and accepted sites of identity-checking and border portal security regimes. In any case, post-Brexit, rebordering Britain was likely to happen anyway in the quest to 'take back control', regardless of the bordering option that was officially endorsed. Britain's border portals, as long-established and accepted sites of people and cargo inspection, were likely to witness an intensification of their border security regimes no matter what transpired at the Irish border.

At the conclusion of the 2016–20 Brexit negotiation process, the rebordering Britain option won out in the form of an 'Irish Sea Border'. From 1 January 2021, Northern Ireland was a constituent part of two diverging unions: the EU and the UK. Ostensibly, the Irish border would remain as was – open and devoid of border inspection and control. However, the four years of truculent Brexit negotiations signalled that years and years and years of EU–UK argument, rankle, and rancour on the Withdrawal Agreement, including the Ireland Northern Ireland Protocol and on the Trade and Cooperation Agreement, lay ahead.[38] For Northern Ireland, would its new experience as a member of two diverging unions mean that it would reap 'the best of both worlds', or would it be stuck 'between a rock and a hard place'? For former British chancellor of the exchequer George Osbourne, the outcome of these agreements meant that 'Northern Ireland is heading for the exit door [of the UK]'. According to Osbourne, 'most here [in Britain] and abroad will not care'.[39]

Notes

1 www.theguardian.com/world/2016/jan/04/swedish-border-controls-oresund-bridge-commuters-refugees (accessed 20/08/2019).
2 See for example www.express.co.uk/news/uk/566380/Britain-braces-more-immigrants-Calais-refugee-camp-Sangatte-2, and www.dailymail.co.uk/news/article-2174296/The-return-Sangatte-Inside-new-mini-migrant-camp-close-Calais.html (both accessed 23/06/2016).
3 http://press.conservatives.com/post/98882674910/david-cameron-speech-to-conservative-party (accessed 02/01/2021).
4 www.maritimeuk.org/about/our-sector/ports/ (accessed 22/05/2020).
5 Gibraltar shares a land border with Spain. However, under the Treaty of Rome (1973) and the UK Act of Accession (1973), Gibraltar is classified as a dependent territory of the UK and not as a member of the UK.
6 www.ft.com/content/268b55ec-a891-11e9-984c-fac8325aaa04 (accessed19/07/2019)

7 *Financial Times*, 25 July 2016 (accessed 28/07/2019).
8 The EU, being a customs union, requires border customs posts to be established between the EU and non-members. This is the case between the EU and Norway which is the subject of the most advanced EU free-trade agreement with a non-member state.
9 HM Government, 2014. *Scotland analysis: Borders and citizenship*. At https://assets.publishing.service.gov.uk/government/uploads/system/uploads/attachment_data/file/274477/scotland_analysis_borders_citizenship.pdf (accessed 12/07/2019).
10 Department of Transport, Tourism and Sport, Republic of Ireland and Department for Infrastructure, Northern Ireland, 2018. 'Public Road Border Crossings Between the Republic of Ireland and Northern Ireland', available at www.infrastructure-ni.gov.uk/sites/default/files/publications/infrastructure/border-crossing-joint-report-final_0.pdf (accessed 15/08/2019).
11 www.thetimes.co.uk/edition/ireland/jacob-rees-mogg-branded-ignorant-over-troubles-policing-border-comment-simon-coveney-spflr8nvz (accessed 12/07/2019).
12 The Legatum Institute also proposed transforming the SEUPB into a border security agency, post-Brexit (Singham et al., 2017, p. 8).
13 Subsequently appointed secretary of state for exiting the European Union (2018), then first secretary of state and secretary of state for foreign and Commonwealth affairs in 2019.
14 *Irish Times*, 11 April 2016. At www.irishtimes.com/news/ireland/irish-news/brexit-could-lead-to-irish-border-controls-tories-warn-1.2605627 (accessed 22/08/2019).
15 https://hansard.parliament.uk/Commons/1922-02-16/debates/d9b2ebfe-12e1-4fc4-b522–2648f173cfe9/IrishFreeState(Agreement)Bill (accessed 30/07/2019).
16 In a comprehensive 'mapping of North–South cooperation', 17 areas of cooperation were identified in the agriculture sector alone, including discussion of common agricultural policy issues, safe use and disposal of animal by-products, cooperation on disease eradication programmes, and cooperation on the safety of the animal feed chain (European Commission, 2019). This sample alludes to the fact that cooperation in this sector is framed by EU policy and law.
17 www.politico.eu/article/brexit-means-good-news-for-irish-smugglers (accessed 10/09/2018).
18 www.irishtimes.com/news/crime-and-law/hard-brexit-will-lead-to-surge-in-cross-border-smuggling-says-report-1.3359154 (accessed 10/09/2018).
19 www.thedetail.tv/articles/loss-of-more-than-40-of-border-stations-prompts-questions-over-future-policing-of-eu-uk-frontier (accessed 02/12/2020).
20 See www.rte.ie/news/brexit/2019/0713/1061902-peace-process and www.irishtimes.com/news/crime-and-law/extra-240-garda%C3%AD-for-border-region-due-to-brexit-1.4065065 (both accessed 02/12/2020).
21 Research conducted in the Central Border Region found this to be the case. Irish and Ulster British communities both appreciated the benefits that two decades of debordering had reaped (Hayward, 2018, p. 77).
22 Part II Exclusion Orders, 3:3, *Prevention of Terrorism (Temporary Provisions) Act 1974* at http://cain.ulst.ac.uk/hmso/pta1974.htm (accessed 19/12/2014).
23 Twenty-two per cent opted for 'neither of these are important to me', and 14 per cent answered 'don't know' (Wellings, 2018).

24 https://lordashcroftpolls.com/2019/10/england-and-the-union (accessed 31/10/2019).
25 https://yougov.co.uk/topics/politics/articles-reports/2019/11/11/four-ten-mainland-britons-dont-care-about-northern (accessed 13/11/2019).
26 www.lbc.co.uk/hot-topics/brexit/brits-would-rather-leave-eu-than-keep-n-ireland/ (accessed 16/07/2019).
27 www.rte.ie/news/elections-2019/2019/0525/1051603-rte-tg4-exit-poll/ (accessed 16/07/2019).
28 https://ec.europa.eu/commission/sites/beta-political/files/draft_withdrawal_agreement_0.pdf (accessed 17/07/2019).
29 It was rejected on 15 January 2019 by 432 to 202 votes. It was rejected for a second time on 12 March 2019 by 391 to 242 votes and rejected a third time on 29 March 2019 by 344 to 286 votes.
30 www.theguardian.com/politics/2019/jul/15/hunt-and-johnson-the-backstop-is-dead-and-cant-be-in-any-eu-deal (accessed 17/07/2019).
31 www.executiveoffice-ni.gov.uk/sites/default/files/publications/execoffice/Letter%20to%20PM%20from%20FM%20%26%20dFM.pdf (accessed 17/07/2019).
32 www.bbc.co.uk/news/av/uk-northern-ireland-42976540/dup-mp-ian-paisley-urges-no-surrender-to-the-eu (accessed 17/07/2019).
33 www.theguardian.com/politics/2019/jul/17/theresa-may-hits-out-at-populists-in-farewell-speech (accessed 18/07/2019).
34 During the presidential election campaign, Biden tweeted, 'Any trade deal between the US and UK must be contingent upon respect for the [Good Friday] Agreement and preventing the return of a hard border. Period', at www.independent.co.uk/news/uk/politics/joe-biden-brexit-good-friday-agreement-trade-deal-b457753.html (accessed 10/11/2020).
35 www.bbc.co.uk/news/uk-politics-55229681 (accessed 08/12/2020).
36 https://ec.europa.eu/info/files/eu-uk-trade-and-cooperation-agreement_en (accessed 26/12/2020).
37 The Draft EU–UK Trade and Cooperation Agreement also committed to the UK leaving the EU's popular Erasmus+ programme. However, the Irish government committed to funding the continued access of Northern Ireland residents to the programme. See www.rte.ie/news/ireland/2020/1226/1186524-erasmus-northern-ireland (accessed 26/12/2020). Additionally, Irish, British, and EU citizens resident in Northern Ireland were to be covered by the Irish government in relation to a reimbursement scheme that would replace the European Health Insurance Card. See www.gov.ie/en/publication/060fdf-northern-ireland (accessed 26/12/2020).
38 Denis MacShane (2019) anticipated that this would be a 'Brexiternity'.
39 www.standard.co.uk/comment/nationalism-union-brexit-b900299.html (accessed 20/01/2021).

5 Borderlessness

Introduction

State borders in Europe continue to matter. Even though their practical functions have been depleted by the process of European integration they remain as stubborn delineators of lives in national imaginations. Binary distinctions between 'self' and 'other', 'us' and 'them', 'friends' and 'enemies', 'here' and 'there', 'home' and 'abroad', 'domestic' and 'foreign', 'threat' and 'security', and 'include' and 'exclude' are justified and embedded by state borders. This is hardly surprising when one considers the investment made in them. Legions have fallen in the defence of state borders or in the heave to remove them.

Conflict over territory has arisen when borders have failed to delineate a 'home place' to the satisfaction of the nation. An ability to mobilise, a justifying ideology, legitimating myths, and interpretive symbols provide the key resources for nationalists to launch political and violent campaigns against their 'Significant Other' over territory. Nationalism prioritises the acquisition and defence of a territorial home with secure borders for the nation. Myths of past victories and defeats legitimate violent conflict over territory. Symbols of flags, languages, songs, commemorations, and the cartographic image of the national territory itself are the touch paper for nationalist political mobilisation over territory. The everyday significance of cultural institutions, such as national museums, universities, and art galleries, for creating and sustaining the place of a bordered territory in the national imagination is also an important consideration. These cultural institutions provide vivid representations of the national home place.

Such a formidable battery of institutional, ideological, and cultural power reinforces the conceptualisation of borderscapes as sites displaying cultural and political complexity, contested discourses and meanings, and struggles over inclusion and exclusion. However, as argued in this book, borderscapes may be manifested as liberating scapes for the cultural and political imagination that provide opportunities for exploring commonalities, respecting differences and reaching for accommodation.

The Irish borderscape has been such a liberating space for intercultural contact, communication and cooperation that has interrogated binary distinctions between Irish nationalists and Ulster British unionists and has envisioned the border as a peace project. However, the vagaries of Brexit exposed the fragility of this liberating space. Brexit involved a retreat to binary bunkers with Remain and Leave (the EU) first among equals. On the island of Ireland, the threat of Brexit rebordering reanimated calls for another binary choice invested in a Border Poll on borderlessness on the island of Ireland and a 'united Ireland' in the EU.

At the outset, this chapter considers the relationship between territory and conflict. It then examines that relationship in the context of the island of Ireland. Efforts to ameliorate conflict over territory on the island through debordering are revisited briefly, as is the rebordering thrust of Brexit. The subsequent momentum for, and resistance to, borderlessness on the island of Ireland via a Border Poll is the central concern of the chapter. The ossifying effect of a binary Brexit and a binary Border Poll on binary manifestations of Irish and Ulster British identities is a key consideration.

Territory and conflict

Territory implies acquisition, ownership, exclusion, and protection, which can provoke emotions of fear, resentment, grievance, and hate. The use of violence becomes plausible in such a malodorous emotional fug (Berezin, 2003, p. 4). Territory comes from the verb *terreor*, 'to frighten', and the noun *territorium*, a place from which people are 'frightened off'. *Territory* and *terrorist* share the same etymology, emphasising the connection between territory and violence (O'Leary, 2001. pp. 5–6).

The human desire for acquisition, ownership, exclusion, and protection, leading to the exercise of social and political power within a territory, has led to its delimitation by borders (Sack, 1986, p. 20). Where there is a dispute over the creation of a modern state territorial border then violence can erupt. The national 'self' prioritises a territorial home and violence, or the threat of violence, has been used readily to acquire or defend that home.

Modern nationalism is a territorially driven ideology. It has prioritised the acquisition and/or defence of 'its' territory, state-building, and the creation of state borders as separation barriers for the nation (Kolossov, 2005, p. 614). National groups that have the ability to mobilise the necessary resources to challenge the 'Significant Other', supported by that motivating ideology, and legitimating myths and symbols, are well primed for conflict over territory (Malešević, 2010, p. 332).

Distinctions have been made between state (civic) nationalism and state-seeking (ethnic) nationalism and imperial (civic) nationalism and anti-imperial (ethnic) nationalism. The violence associated with nationalism is often attributed to the state-seekers and the anti-imperialists. These 'hot' nationalists, fortified by grievance-driven nationalism, are assumed to have a predisposition for conflict over territory. Their fallen martyrs can be mobilised and rendered powerful emotion agents for mobilisation against the 'Significant Other'. However, if civic nationalists' cultural distinctiveness, territorial integrity and political autonomy are threatened they too can become 'hot' (Spencer and Wollman, 1998; Brown, 1999; Hutchinson, 2005, p. 147). Its pursuit of national territorial autonomy has cast modern nationalism of whatever hue as the ideology that is most often charged with the construction of violent conflict over territory.

The legacy of Irish border conflict

In modern Ireland, political and violent means have been employed for the purpose of achieving national goals, including that of acquiring a territorial home. For Irish nationalists, the political path often coincided with the threat of violence. Daniel O'Connell's peaceful 'monster meetings' for Catholic emancipation, between 1843 and 1845, implied violent threat. Charles Stewart Parnell's association with the Land League's mobilisation of the Irish peasantry later in the nineteenth century blurred the line between political and violent revolutionary paths (Nic Dháibhéid and Reid, 2010). On the Ulster British side, the threat of violence to support political opposition to Home Rule for Ireland was clearly demonstrated by the creation of the Ulster Volunteer Force (UVF) and its connection to Edward Carson's (Ulster) Unionist Party,[1] so much so that an authoritative book on the UVF is entitled *Carson's Army: The Ulster Volunteer Force, 1910–1922* (Bowman, 2007). Later in the twentieth century, Democratic Unionist Party (DUP) leader, the Reverend Ian Paisley, was tempted to repeat the trick, most conspicuously at the launch of the loyalist paramilitary organisation Ulster Resistance (Bruce, 1995).

Ireland's two main political parties, Fianna Fáil and Fine Gael, were the products of violent revolutionary politics of the early twentieth century. Two Fianna Fáil leaders and Taoisigh (prime ministers), Éamon de Valera and Seán Lemass, had been active Irish Republican Army (IRA) insurgents in the Irish War of Independence, 1919–21. However, Sinn Féin's 'Armalite[2] and ballot paper' rallying cry of the 1980s, reflecting its intimate relationship with the IRA, was the most explicit expression of 'the voice and the sword' in Irish politics of the post-partition era (Nic Dháibhéid and Reid, 2010). Sinn Féin became the sole standard-bearer of the anti-partitionist 'voice and the sword' strategy. However, as political violence took hold in Northern Ireland after 1969, a partitionist inclination became perceptible in southern politics and society with a 26-county Irish state nationalism figure-headed by the public intellectual Conor Cruise O'Brien[3] (O'Brien, 1972, 1980; O'Halloran, 1987; O'Callaghan, 2018).

After partition, Northern Ireland became consolidated as a 'Protestant state for a Protestant people', with the Ulster Protestant British unionist community exerting ethnonational dominance over the Irish Catholic nationalist community (Anderson, 2008; McKenna, 2016). Ulster British ethnonationalist dominance manifested itself in discrimination in the allocation of public-sector housing, in employment, as well as in the denial of political rights to Irish Catholics through gerrymandering to ensure an Ulster British unionist hegemony in city councils, most notably in Derry/Londonderry with its large Irish Catholic majority (O'Hearn, 1983). Such discrimination and inequality contributed to the emergence of the civil rights movement which organised mass protests and actions of civil disobedience. The Ulster British unionist hegemony – and Northern Ireland as an exclusive Ulster British home place – was being challenged. Political and violent unionist and loyalist reaction followed, as did resurgent republican violence and the question of partition reemerged (Kennedy-Pipe, 2013).

Bordering Ireland, enacted half a century earlier by the British government, became the key issue of the post-1969 Troubles. For Irish nationals, the border was the scar through the indivisible island and a barrier to the consolidation of their national home place. For the Ulster British, the border became an existential barrier – the last line of defence – that maintained their identity, position, and privilege in their six-county home place of Northern Ireland that they affectionately referred to as 'Our Wee Country'. In the Ulster British imagination, the 'Brits Out' refrain of republicans during the Troubles reinforced the necessity of the border as a barrier.

From rebordering to a border poll

Good Friday Agreement politics and debordering the Irish border helped calm the unionist–nationalist territorial dispute. The agreement was significant because, for the first time since partition, Irish republicans entered power-sharing government with Ulster British unionists in Northern Ireland, an entity that they had considered alien and illegitimate. The Ulster British unionists, meanwhile, abandoned their long-held claim on Northern Ireland as exclusively 'theirs'. The agreement required political parties across the spectrum to de-emphasise the unionist–nationalist territorial dispute.

Debordering was also significant because the border was the central issue of the Troubles: republicans wanted to destroy the border, unionists wished to preserve and reinforce it. O'Dowd and McCall (2008) emphasise the debordering role of the EU and the North–South institutional dimension in the Good Friday Agreement. However, throughout this period the consociational, trans-state form of governance provided by agreement was institutionally fragile and prone to suspension when disagreements arose between Irish nationalist and Ulster British unionist protagonists.

In January 2017, the Northern Ireland institutions were suspended in the midst of a corruption scandal, and disagreements between the DUP and Sinn Féin over the status of the Irish language, abortion rights, and same-sex marriage in Northern Ireland. When the institutions were reactivated three years later (in January 2020), the new Sinn Féin leader, Mary Lou McDonald, while supportive of the reactivation, stated that the overriding objective of Sinn Féin was ending partition, a 'united Ireland' and borderlessness on the island: 'we will . . . continue to work for Irish reunification' (McDonald, 2020). Sinn Féin emerged from the 2020 general election in the South as the state's largest party in terms of first preference votes. However, the party went into opposition after a historic coalition government was formed by Fianna Fáil, Fine Gael, and the Green Party.

The Brexit negotiations from 2016 to 2020 placed debordering on the island of Ireland in question. They also reopened the territorial question and placed Irish reunification back on the political agenda. Throughout the years of those negotiations, the possibility of rebordering the Irish border remained in the frame. Consequently, questions of territoriality in Ireland, and the reunification of the island became omnipresent.

Right from the off, Sinn Féin called for a reunification referendum and launched their case on the basis of the majority Remain vote in Northern Ireland where 56 per cent voted to remain in the EU. In an op-ed in the *New York Times* published shortly after the referendum vote, Gerry Adams (2016), then Sinn Féin leader, claimed that Brexit offered 'a reason and an opportunity' for a referendum where Northern Ireland citizens could decide whether they 'wanted to be part of a Britain outside the European Union or belong to a unified Irish state in Europe'.

In a Brexit policy paper, Sinn Féin explicitly stated that 'the prospect of the North being removed from the EU against the will of the people, and the return of a hard border in Ireland, has brought the issue of Irish reunification firmly back onto the political agenda' (2016, p. 1). According to John Brewer, Brexit prompted Sinn Féin to realign its strategy shifting 'from power sharing in the North of Ireland to reunification of the Island' (2018, p. 171). This 'strategic realignment' can be explained by the fact that the republican objective of a 'united Ireland' moved from the aspirational to the possible in the Brexit context (Doyle and Connolly, 2019, p. 87). It was encouraged by the party's electoral successes North and South and by some opinion polls on a 'united Ireland'.

Meanwhile, other Irish national parties continued to prioritise the need to achieve 'an agreed Ireland' or 'Shared Island' over a 'united Ireland'. The nebulous term 'Agreed Ireland' was most closely associated with former Social Democratic and Labour Party (SDLP) leader John Hume and implied nationalist–unionist consent on the island of Ireland for constitutional arrangements and structures of governance. Thus, the 1998 Good Friday Agreement arguably delivered an 'Agreed Ireland' because consent was given via referenda on the agreement, North and South.[4]

In 2020, Taoiseach and Fianna Fáil leader Micheál Martin introduced the Fianna Fáil/Fine Gael/Green Party coalition government's policy of a 'Shared Island'[5] and its 'consensus approach' while criticising Sinn Féin's push for a Border Poll.[6] According to the Tánaiste[7] and Fine Gael leader Leo Varadkar, an 'Agreed Ireland' meant building 'a set of relationships that we can all be happy with'. For him, a 'united Ireland' should only happen with the consent of Ulster British unionists.[8] Yet the flipside of Ulster British unionist consent is a veto on a 'united Ireland'.

The DUP was opposed to the Good Friday Agreement. Although the DUP subsequently participated in the operation of the institutions of governance that the agreement provided the party was steadfast in its hostility to the agreement's North–South dimension and remained committed to frustrating the operation of the North South Ministerial Council. The DUP has enjoyed by far the largest share of the unionist vote in Northern Ireland since the agreement.[9] From an 'Agreed Ireland' or 'Shared Island' political perspective, nothing happens without Ulster British unionist, and probably DUP, consent. Therefore, even if majorities of the electorate in the North and in the South voted for a 'united Ireland' in a Border Poll, the 'Agreed Ireland' or 'Shared Island' consent benchmark would determine that a 'united Ireland' could not become a reality without Ulster British unionist, and probably DUP, consent.

In the Brexit context, however, the 'united Ireland' agenda was boosted from a wholly unexpected source. When Taoiseach, then Fine Gael leader Enda Kenny – not normally viewed as a 'united Irelander' – played a crucial role in successfully persuading his European counterparts in the EC to include a clause that stated that Northern Ireland could automatically enter the EU in the event of Irish reunification. A statement published in April 2017 explicitly recognised the possibility of a united Ireland, where Northern Ireland would automatically be a member of the EU:

> The European Council acknowledges that the Good Friday Agreement expressly provides for an agreed mechanism whereby a united Ireland

> may be brought about through peaceful and democratic means. In this regard, the European Council acknowledges that, in accordance with international law, the entire territory of such a united Ireland would thus be part of the European Union.
>
> (European Parliament, 2017)

It is unlikely that such a statement supporting a united Ireland would have been made without Brexit. Thus, Brexit may be regarded as promoting, at the EU level, borderlessness on the island of Ireland (Castan Pinos and McCall, 2021).

Border Poll

When the Good Friday Agreement was delivered in 1998, debordering rather than borderlessness on the island of Ireland was the priority. If anything, borderlessness and a united Ireland were not on the political agenda since the Irish national political parties, including Sinn Féin, committed to the agreement and its version of an 'Agreed Ireland'. Additionally, Articles 2 and 3 of Bunreacht na hÉireann|Constitution of Ireland were amended to emphasise respect for identities and traditions and remove reference to the reintegration of the territory. However, the intervening decades revealed an electorally strengthening Irish community vis-à-vis the Ulster British community in Northern Ireland with Sinn Féin benefitting. The Brexit bombshell 'blew the bloody doors off' – to paraphrase Charlie Croker (Michael Caine) in the film *The Italian Job* – and catapulted the issues of territoriality and borders back onto the political agendas of Britain and Ireland.

The Good Friday Agreement itself stipulated the conditions for a referendum on a 'united Ireland':

> [T]he Secretary of State [for Northern Ireland] shall exercise the power [to hold a Border Poll] if at any time it appears likely to him that a majority of those voting would express a wish that Northern Ireland should cease to be part of the United Kingdom and form part of a united Ireland.
>
> (The Agreement, Schedule 1[10])

As such, it appeared that the secretary of state for Northern Ireland was solely invested with the power to call such a poll. However, this appearance was complicated somewhat by the UK High Court judicial review with respect to *An Application for Judicial Review by Raymond McCord* (GIR 10679) which was delivered on 28 June 2018.[11] Legally, the judicial review confirmed the power of the secretary of state to call a Border Poll. However, Mark Bassett and Colin Harvey highlight the review's distinction between the 'broad discretionary power' of the secretary of state to call a poll and the 'duty' to call such a poll if there appeared to be a majority of voters in Northern Ireland in favour of a 'united Ireland'. For Bassett and Harvey, that 'duty' even extended to ensuring Northern Ireland's continued membership of the EU as a part of a 'united Ireland' in the event of a 'no deal' Brexit (2019, pp. 5–6). Nevertheless, legally and politically, it is difficult to dislodge the primacy of 'the likelihood of a majority of voters voting for a united Ireland' as the guiding principle for calling a Border Poll (Whysall, 2019).

Opinion polls on a 'united Ireland' provide the critical evidence for that likelihood, and no matter what they say, politicians are slaves to opinion polls. Reliable polls conducted prior to the EU–UK 'deal or no deal' deadline of 31 December 2020 indicated an even split in Northern Ireland between those favouring Northern Ireland remaining in the UK and those preferring a 'united Ireland'. For example, a LucidTalk poll for *The Detail*, conducted between 31 January and 3 February 2020, and involving 1896 respondents in Northern Ireland and 1171 in Ireland, found that 46.8 per cent of Northern Ireland voters would vote for Northern Ireland to remain in the UK, 45.4 per cent would vote for a 'united Ireland', while 7.8 per cent were undecided. In Ireland, it found that 73.1 per cent of respondents would vote for Northern Ireland to be part of a 'united Ireland', 10.2 per cent would vote for Northern Ireland to remain in the UK, while 16.7 per cent were undecided. A referendum on a 'united Ireland' taking place within the next 10 years was supported by a majority in both jurisdictions. The results prompted Colin Harvey, a leading advocate for a 'united Ireland' referendum, to pronounce: 'It increasingly looks like support for the current constitutional arrangements is on a knife-edge. That is simply remarkable. It shakes the legitimacy of the foundations of the existing constitutional order'. For Harvey, the results confirmed that 'this island is heading towards these referendums. Whether that is within five or 10 years is a matter for political debate. There is no excuse for avoiding the work involved in managing the potential for constitutional change that will arise'.[12]

The first and foremost question to be addressed on constitutional change and borderless on the island of Ireland regards the configuration of an all-Ireland state: Would a unified Ireland be a unitary state, a federation, or a confederation? Crucially, would constitutional change involve Northern Ireland continuing in the form of a federal or confederal power-sharing region of a 'united Ireland'? The Good Friday Agreement provides, and advocates, for a North–South, East–West institutional template for the transition to the latter:

> It is accepted that all of the institutional and constitutional arrangements – an Assembly in Northern Ireland, a North/South Ministerial Council, implementation bodies, a British-Irish Council and a British-Irish Intergovernmental Conference and any amendments to British Acts of Parliament and the Constitution of Ireland – are interlocking and interdependent and that in particular the functioning of the Assembly and the North/South Council are so closely inter-related that the success of each depends on that of the other.
>
> (The Agreement, Declaration of Support, 5)[13]

Transition to a 'united Ireland' could involve enhanced remits for the cross-border connecting institutions, namely the North South Ministerial Council and its Implementation Bodies, the British–Irish Council and the British–Irish Intergovernmental Conference.

Prior to a Border Poll, all these options and issues would require exploration in a constitutional convention or forum or assembly to inform the questions posed in that referendum[14] (Doyle, 2020).

The In-betweeners

The 'non-aligned' In-betweeners in Northern Ireland are pivotal in a 'united Ireland' referendum. By 2019, the In-betweeners – neither Ulster British unionist nor Irish nationalist – share of the vote in Northern Ireland reached a high of approximately 20 per cent. The Irish national and Ulster British share was approximately 40 per cent each. The Alliance Party of Northern Ireland and the Green Party in Northern Ireland are the principal 'non-aligned' In-betweener political parties.

Brexit has, however, challenged In-betweener non-aligned convictions. Polling indicates that half of Alliance voters would vote for a 'united Ireland', a third are undecided, and a fifth would vote for Northern Ireland to remain in the UK.[15] Meanwhile, the Green Party stood aside in favour of pro-Remain (in the EU) candidates in the 2019 UK General Election, notably in North Belfast (won by Sinn Féin) and South Belfast (won by the SDLP), indicating that the Green's would support a 'united Ireland' in the EU.

The Alliance Party share of the vote rose dramatically from 8 per cent in the 2017 general election to 17 per cent in the 2019 UK general election. In 2020 the Alliance Party leadership stated that there was no case for a Border Poll but recognised that the situation was 'very fluid'. Alliance concluded that 'there is space for a civilised, rational and evidence-based discussions on the issue'.[16] Previously, the party had indicated a tentative interest in a citizens' assembly for conducting such discussions.[17]

According to Jon Tonge,

> [a]lliance oscillates between acting primarily as a political umbrella, a political shelter under which people of differing political ideologies and religious backgrounds and constitutional perspectives comfortably co-exist and a more radical vehicle, rejecting unionism and nationalism outright and viewing both as regressive entities needing to be usurped by a common identity (neutral Northern Irishness).
>
> (2020, p. 465)

Brexit and a binary Border Poll upsets this delicate balancing act because the binary choice is between the constitutional preference of Irish nationalism (a 'united Ireland') and that of Ulster British unionism (Northern Ireland remaining in the UK). However, the Alliance Party's participation in a constitutional convention on the configuration of a 'united Ireland' offers the party wriggle room because it could then argue for constitutional change involving Northern Ireland continuing in the form of a federal or confederal power-sharing region of Ireland, something potentially compatible with both 'political umbrella' and radical 'Northern Ireland' versions of itself.

(Dis)United Ireland

For the Ulster British, the recognition of Britishness *in* Northern Ireland has necessitated the recognition of the Britishness *of* Northern Ireland. This position has excluded the Irish and Irishness in Northern Ireland. and served to perpetuate Irish–Ulster British political and cultural conflict. It also acts as a cultural stumbling block for a constitutional transition to a borderless 'united Ireland' wherein Northern Ireland becomes a part of that EU member state. Borderlessness in a 'united Ireland' as an EU member state is likely to further animate questions posed in the realm of cultural politics, namely Whose culture shall be the official one, and whose shall be subordinated? What culture shall be regarded as worthy of display, and which shall be hidden? Whose history shall be remembered, and whose is forgotten? What images of social life shall be projected, and which shall be marginalised? What voices shall be heard, and which silenced? and Who is representing whom, and on what basis? (Jordan and Weedon, 1995, p. 4).

With the implementation of the 1998 agreement, Ulster British unionist leaders maintained that a concerted effort was being made to undermine the Britishness of Northern Ireland and that the region was becoming a 'cold place for unionists'.[18] For example, the inclusive symbol of the new Police Service of Northern Ireland was interpreted by some Ulster British unionists as a watering-down of the Britishness of Northern Ireland. Reconfiguring the cultural representation of Northern Ireland either as a neutral public space or as one that reflects the region's Britishness and Irishness, had a detrimental effect on Ulster British attitudes towards the 1998 agreement and its implementation. For the Ulster British, their culture was being subordinated, regarded as not worthy of display, and threatened with silence.

Languages (Gaelic and Ulster-Scots), parades, and flags have been the primary cultural resources for the pursuance of a culture war in Northern Ireland. The Ulster British culture of parading and flag-flying has traditionally served to symbolically assert Ulster British territorial control in Northern Ireland. After the Good Friday Agreement, Ulster British leaders interpreted cultural politics as a key battleground for their identity and the identity of Northern Ireland generally. They recognised that, in the aftermath of the agreement's territorial compromise, cultural politics determined the way in which Northern Ireland is represented, particularly in relation to Ireland (McCall, 2005).

There is no reason to believe that a 'united Ireland' and borderlessness would bring the Irish–Ulster British culture war to an end. Quite the opposite. A 'united Ireland' in the EU would entail the euro replacing the British pound as the currency of Northern Ireland, a daily reminder of 'loss of Britishness' and one likely to be exploited by Ulster British emotion entrepreneurs. It is likely to provoke an intensification of Ulster British parading, bonfire burning, and flag-flying in an effort to project the Ulster British self-image, culturally mark 'their' territorial home place of Northern Ireland, and perform the 'border in the mind' (Gormley-Heenan and Aughey, 2017). However, for some, like DUP leader Arlene Foster, borderlessness on the island of Ireland would provoke thoughts of leaving the home place altogether: 'If it were to happen, I'm not sure that I would be able to continue to live here. I would feel so strongly about it. I would probably have to move'.[19]

The British/Irish commentator Dennis Kennedy (2014) entertained the idea of a federal Ireland and the place of the Ulster British community in it. For Kennedy, as well as a new constitution, to reflect the 'new Ireland', the state would have to undertake cultural 'adjustments' including the jettisoning of the Irish national flag, the national anthem, the Gaelic language as 'the first national language', the names of railway stations,[20] and Irish neutrality. A long and challenging shopping list for Ireland in what Kennedy himself dismissed as an exercise in 'fantacising'.

In 2018, Peter Robinson, former DUP leader and former first minister of Northern Ireland, stood out as an established Ulster British voice publicly willing to entertain the possibility of a 'united Ireland'. He called for the need to prepare for the possibility of a 'united Ireland', adding, 'I don't expect my own house to burn down but I still insure it because it could happen'. He thought that the Ulster British unionist community generally would accept the result of a Border Poll that delivered a 'united Ireland' but that it would require 'protections' in the new dispensation.[21] Robinson was lambasted by other unionist politicians for his intervention. His DUP colleague Sammy Wilson, MP, issued a telling repost, steeped in the conflict binary of the Ulster British home place and the antagonistic Irish republican 'Significant Other', when he opined that Robinson's was an 'invitation to republican arsonists to come in and burn *our* house down' (author's emphasis).[22]

The 1998 agreement made provision for a Border Poll every seven years after the first one (The Agreement, Schedule 1[23]). Alan Whysall argued that 'if the result was a narrow negative, it might mean that the focus of politics would thereafter change radically away from making things work in Northern Ireland towards preparing the battle lines for further polls at seven-year intervals' (2019, p. 14). On the other hand, a narrow vote for a 'united Ireland' could be met with Ulster British loyalist violence. However, such loyalist violence would be fruitless politically because the Good Friday Agreement does not provide for Northern Ireland with a route back to the UK. Taken together, the agreement's dice are firmly loaded in favour of the movement towards a 'united Ireland'. As such, Whysall concludes that 'Northern Ireland's membership of the UK is always conditional, but a switch to a united Ireland is definitive' (2019, p. 10).

Conclusion

The swan song of the late SDLP deputy leader and deputy first minister of Northern Ireland Seamus Mallon was his book titled *A Shared Home Place* (2019). For much of the last century, the territorial conflict between Irish nationalists and Ulster British unionists on the island of Ireland built separate home places, North and South. Northern Ireland as the Ulster British home place was a 'cold house' for Irish people. However, the outworking of Europeanisation and the 1998 Good Friday Agreement held out the promise of an Irish/Ulster British shared home place through debordering, power-sharing, and cultural parity in Northern Ireland. Brexit rebordering, and its ossifying effect on binary conceptions of Irish and Ulster British identities, seriously undermined the shared home-place enterprise.

Brexit also energised the push for borderlessness on the island of Ireland through another binary exercise: a Border Poll.[24] In that poll, it would appear that the In-betweeners in Northern Ireland – neither Irish nationalist nor Ulster British unionist – would have the decisive call. For them, the Brexit diminution of their European citizenships rights and identity was likely to be an important factor in the choice that they made. A 'united Ireland' would secure those rights and identity through the automatic re-entry of Northern Ireland to the EU as a part of an existing member state: Ireland.

Should a Border Poll deliver a 'united Ireland', the quest to secure a shared home place would necessitate the continuation of Northern Ireland as a federal or confederal unit as the bottom line. However, there is no reason to believe that it would resolve the Irish–Ulster British culture war. Au contraire. A loss of Britishness would be keenly felt by the Ulster British. Northern Ireland would no longer be a part of the UK, and moreover, it would be a part of a 'united Ireland' in the EU. Everyday symbols such as the British pound would be jettisoned and replaced by the euro. A symbolic backlash by the Ulster British could be expected, with an investment made in the cultural marking of 'their' territorial home place. However, a violent reaction would be politically fruitless because, in the event of a Border Poll that delivered a 'united Ireland', there would be no route back to bordering on the island of Ireland, no route back for Northern Ireland as a member of the UK.

Notes

1 Mirrored by the formation of the Irish Volunteers in 1913 with which the Irish Party eventually became involved (Reid, 2010).
2 Armalite refers to "ArmaLite", a US rifle brand that was the IRA gun of choice.
3 In later life the 'Cruiser', as he was popularly known, became a unionist, and then a 'united Irelander' albeit with Ulster British interests prioritised.
4 Seventy-one per cent voted 'Yes' in Northern Ireland, and 95 per cent voted 'Yes' in Ireland. See www.ark.ac.uk/elections/fref98.htm (accessed 21/10/2020).
5 The 'Shared Island' policy commanded a budget of €500m (2020–5) for the delivery of cross-border and all-island infrastructure and other initiatives. See www.gov.ie/en/press-release/2c97f-taoiseach-statement-on-shared-island-fund/ (accessed 21/10/2020).
6 www.irishtimes.com/news/politics/shared-island-united-ireland-question-edges-into-mainstream-political-debate-1.4345768 (accessed 21/10/2020).
7 Deputy prime minister.
8 www.irishnews.com/paywall/tsb/irishnews/irishnews/irishnews//news/republicofirelandnews/2018/01/02/news/varadkar-i-aspire-to-united-island-and-hume-s-agreed-ireland–1223131/content.html (accessed 21/10/2020).
9 In the 2019 UK general election, the DUP secured 30.6 per cent of the vote. Its nearest unionist party rival, the Ulster Unionist Party, received 11.7 per cent. See www.bbc.co.uk/news/election/2019/results/northern_ireland (accessed 21/10/2020).
10 https://assets.publishing.service.gov.uk/government/uploads/system/uploads/attachment_data/file/136652/agreement.pdf (accessed 20/07/2020).

11 https://brexitlawni.org/assets/uploads/Our-Shared-Island-A-Paper-on-Unity-CCG-2019.pdf (accessed 07/12/2020).
12 https://thedetail.tv/articles/a-majority-favour-a-border-poll-on-the-island-of-ireland-in-the-next-10-years (accessed 10/08/2020).
13 https://assets.publishing.service.gov.uk/government/uploads/system/uploads/attachment_data/file/136652/agreement.pdf (accessed 20/07/2020).
14 A good start was made by the Joint Committee on the Implementation of the Good Friday Agreement, Houses of the Oireachtas (Ireland's national parliament), by the adoption of a sprawling, detailed 2017 report titled *Brexit and the Future of Ireland: Uniting Ireland & Its People in Peace & Prosperity* (32/JCIGFA/02), available at https://webarchive.oireachtas.ie/parliament/media/committees/implementationofthegoodfridayagreement/jcigfa2016/brexit-and-the-future-of-ireland.pdf (accessed 01/08/2020). Regarding the precise preparation and process required for a Border Poll, see the Working Group on Unification Referendums on the Island of Ireland, 2020. *Interim Report*, November. London: The Constitution Unit, University College London, available at www.ucl.ac.uk/constitution-unit/sites/constitution-unit/files/wgurii_interim_report_nov_2020.pdf (accessed 27/11/2020).
15 www.thedetail.tv/articles/irish-unity-and-disunity (accessed 10/08/2020).
16 www.irishtimes.com/news/ireland/irish-news/no-current-case-for-united-ireland-border-poll-alliance-party-1.4196502 (accessed 10/08/2020).
17 www.thetimes.co.uk/article/alliance-party-open-to-citizens-assembly-on-border-poll-ncpwz5v9h (accessed 10/08/2020).
18 For example see 'Northern Ireland: A Cold Place for Unionists' in the *Irish Times*, 14 and 15 January 2002.
19 www.belfasttelegraph.co.uk/news/northern-ireland/dup-leader-arlene-foster-would-not-assimilate-in-a-united-ireland-36947067.html (accessed 11/08/2020).
20 Fifteen of which were named after executed leaders of the 1916 rebellion. See www.thejournal.ie/irish-rail-1916-2-2744978-Apr2016/ (accessed 20/09/2020).
21 www.irishtimes.com/news/ireland/irish-news/north-should-prepare-for-united-ireland-possibility-ex-dup-leader-1.3578620 (accessed 05/12/2020).
22 www.bbc.co.uk/news/uk-northern-ireland-45000495 (accessed 05/12/2020).
23 https://assets.publishing.service.gov.uk/government/uploads/system/uploads/attachment_data/file/136652/agreement.pdf (accessed 20/07/2020).
24 In his book, Mallon favoured the idea of 'parallel consent', whereby a sizeable percentage of the Ulster British unionist vote – up to 50 per cent – would be required for the confirmation of a 'united Ireland' and the delivery of a 'shared home place'. Problematically, his approach speaks to ethnocracy rather than democracy.

Conclusion

The island of Ireland has experienced a century of 'the border'. Throughout that century, Irish nationalists maintained that the border was an unjustifiable partition of the 'indivisible Island' (Gallagher, 1957). The Ulster British unionists, on the other hand, came to see the border as a necessary barrier between two separate – Irish and Ulster British – home places (Heslinga, 1962). Problematically, the Ulster British home place also housed a sizeable and growing Irish national population for whom it was a 'cold house'.

After partition, a process of bordering reinforced the border between Northern Ireland and the Irish state. State-building on either side of the border, enmity between the Ulster British and Irish national communities, and political elites and their respective media, as well as political violence, fortified the bordering process.

Trading on perceptions of threat and insecurity posed by the Irish nationalist 'Significant Other' Ulster British unionist leaders rejected any countervailing effort to develop institutionalised North–South cooperation. The apotheosis of bordering was the result of the British counter-offensive against the cross-border activities of Irish republican insurgents during the 1970s and 1980s. Border crossing points were obstructed or destroyed by the British security forces and key cross-border arterial routes were securitised. Irish republican insurgents and British security personnel became locked in a desperate, deadly dance that infused this border zone of dystopia with fear, loathing, and trepidation.

In the 1990s, some optimistic souls saw a way through this bordering conundrum by way of a 'postmodern', 'post-sovereignty' European space wherein territory would lose its salience as a political determinant (Kearney, 1996; McCall, 1998). Debordering, involving the dismantlement of physical border infrastructure and the promotion of intergovernmental and cross-border cooperation, did indeed commence on the island of Ireland in the 1990s thanks to Europeanisation and the Irish Peace Process.

British–Irish intergovernmental cooperation was kick-started by the accession of Ireland and the UK to the EC space in 1973 and entered firmly into the embrace of the process of Europeanisation. The first product of British–Irish intergovernmental cooperation was the 1985 Anglo-Irish Agreement which involved the Irish government in the governance of Northern Ireland. The 1998 Good Friday Agreement delivered a North–South dimension which institutionally established debordering via the North South Ministerial Council, Secretariat, and Implementation Bodies for the island of Ireland. However, initial Ulster British unionist political leaders' acquiescence to 'North-Southery' – to use their pejorative term – deteriorated into obstruction, and continuing Irish–Ulster British political and cultural conflict lead to the stagnation of these all-Ireland institutions.

In the Irish borderscape itself, the border zone of dystopia of the 1970s and 1980s was transformed into one that, in the 1990s and 2000s, embodied the conflict transformation trinity of contact, communication, and cooperation across a border. Contact, communication, and cooperation, together with the free movement of people unencumbered by a border security regime, transformed the Irish borderscape. It became a cultural borderscape for challenging binary distinctions between 'self' and 'other', 'us' and 'them', 'friends' and 'enemies', 'here' and 'there', 'home' and 'abroad', 'domestic' and 'foreign', 'threat' and 'security', and 'include' and 'exclude'.

The Peace programmes for Northern Ireland and the border counties of Ireland (1995–2027) have been intrinsic to that transformation. Sports, history, and languages have been key cultural resources mobilised to provide entry points for people to engage on a cross-border, cross-community (Irish–Ulster British) basis. That engagement addressed Ulster British conceptions of threat and insecurity. That engagement confronted Irish–Ulster British conflict antagonisms and charted a conflict transformation course towards respect for cultural difference and the recognition of commonalities.

Prior to the Brexit referendum thunderbolt of 2016, the Irish cultural borderscape was already vulnerable because of British–Irish intergovernmental complacency and neglect and a severe economic downturn. Some solace was to be found in the EU's unwavering commitment to the Peace programmes, extending them to 2027. However, it was the Brexit referendum on the withdrawal of the UK from the EU – resulting in a majority of 52 per cent in favour of the United Kingdom of Great Britain and Northern Ireland exiting the EU – that turned the page in a debordering–rebordering–borderlessness nexus on the island of Ireland.

Brexit presented the possibility of rebordering the Irish border through the re-securitisation of cross-border arterial routes, the re-closure of secondary cross-border roads, the reinstatement of border security infrastructure, and the introduction of mobile border security patrols. That possibility, animated during the four years of tortuous Brexit negotiations between 2016 and 2020 – on the terms of UK withdrawal and the post-Brexit EU–UK relationship – re-dramatised the power dynamic and conflictual relationship between Ulster British unionist and Irish nationalist ideologies.

Ultimately, Brexit was navigated by British prime minister Boris Johnson, his ministers Michael Gove and Dominic Raab, and the leader of the House of Commons, Jacob Rees-Mogg. With a potent combination of indolence, post-imperial delusion, and a fulsome slathering of hyperbole, this Brexiter riff-raff was in command of the good ship Britannia as it sailed towards a rocky Brexit shoreline with Hibernia caught in its drag.

In the context of the UK withdrawal from the EU, there was one alternative to re-bordering the island of Ireland: reborder Britain by establishing an 'Irish Sea Border'. This was what transpired in the Ireland/Northern Ireland Protocol attached to the Withdrawal Agreement. The advantage of an 'Irish Sea Border' was that it would be relatively simple to establish because of its focus on a limited number of border portals – seaports and airports – that were long-accepted sites of people and cargo inspection and of border security regimes. The disadvantage was that an Ulster British perception of threat, insecurity, and abandonment by their mainland – Britain – could ignite political agitation and violent mayhem anew.

For Paul Teague, 'there is no Brexit solution that will create a mutual gains bargain between nationalism and unionism' (2019, p. 697). This zero-sum game scenario, which diverged entirely from the inclusive nature of the Good Friday Agreement, paved the way for the re-emergence and entrenchment of the territorial conflict in Northern Ireland. One solution placed the 'In-betweeners' centre frame: a 'united Ireland'. Neither Ulster British unionist nor Irish nationalist, the In-betweeners – mainly supporters of the Alliance Party and the Green Party – began to command sufficient electoral heft in Northern Ireland to be the decisive factor in a Border Poll. For them, Brexit's threat to their European citizenship rights and identity was likely to be a persuasive factor in voting for a 'united Ireland', not least because it would guarantee the immediate re-entry of Northern Ireland to the EU as a part of an existing member state.

The timeline trajectory of this book runs through bordering after partition, Europeanisation and Irish peace process inspired debordering from 1992, Brexit rebordering from 2016, leading inexorably to the reinvigoration of the political campaign for borderlessness on the island of Ireland. Borderlessness, in itself, would create a whole new set of formidable economic,[1] political, and identity challenges. First and foremost, how can the Ulster British community be accommodated in a 'united Ireland'?

In the oeuvre of the great English songwriter Nick Lowe rests one of his gems '(What's So Funny 'Bout) Peace, Love, and Understanding'.

Absolutely nothing when it has been so hard fought for over the course of two decades in the Irish borderscape, on the island of Ireland and between Britain and Ireland. What would really be not so funny is if the peace, love, and understanding gains made during the halcyon decades of the British–Irish peace process were to dissipate in the mists of an ersatz, post-imperial Brexit quest for British global glory. If a borderless Ireland in the EU is realised as a result, it is likely that the fight for peace, love, and understanding between the Irish and the Ulster British will have to begin all over again. That will require a strong and stable British–Irish intergovernmental relationship. Also required will be the EU, as before.

Note

1 The economic challenges of, and prospects for, a 'united Ireland' are discussed in https://ideas.repec.org/p/tcd/tcduee/tep0619.html, and https://cain.ulster.ac.uk/issues/unification/hubner_2015-08.pdf (accessed 12/12/2020).

References

Adams, Gerry, 2016. 'Brexit and Irish Unity', in *The New York Times*, 12 July, Available at www.nytimes.com/2016/07/12/opinion/brexit-and-irish-unity.html (accessed 13/01/2020).

Amilhat Szary, Anne-Laure and Frédéric Giraut, 2015. 'Borderities: The Politics of Contemporary Mobile Borders', pp. 1–19 in Anne-Laure Amilhat Szary and Frédéric Giraut (eds.), *Borderities and the Politics of Contemporary Mobile Borders*. Basingstoke: Palgrave Macmillan.

Amoore, Louise, 2006. 'Biometric Borders: Governing Mobilities in the War on Terror', pp. 336–351 in *Political Geography*, vol. 25, no. 3.

Anderson, James, 2008. 'Partition, Consociation, Border-crossing: Some Lessons from the National Conflict in Ireland/Northern Ireland', pp. 85–104 in *Nations and Nationalism*, vol. 14, no. 1.

Anderson, James, 2018. 'Ireland's Borders, Brexit Centre-Stage: A Commentary', pp. 255–269 in *Space and Polity*, vol. 2, no. 2.

Anderson, James and Liam O'Dowd, 2007. 'Imperial Disintegration and the Creation of the Irish Border: Imperialism and Nationalism 1885–1925', pp. 295–308 in *Political Geography*, vol. 26, no. 8.

Anderson, Malcolm and Eberhard Bort, 2001. *The Frontiers of the European Union*. Basingstoke: Palgrave Macmillan.

Andreas, Peter, 2003. 'Redrawing the Line: Borders and Security in the Twenty-First Century', pp. 78–111 in *International Security*, vol. 28, no. 2.

Arthur, Paul, 2000. *Special Relationships: Britain, Ireland and the Northern Ireland Problem*. Belfast: Blackstaff.

Aughey, Arthur, 1989. *Under Siege: Ulster Unionism and the Anglo-Irish Agreement*. London: Hurst & Co.

Bassett, Mark and Colin Harvey, 2019. 'The Future of our Shared Island: A Paper on the Logistical and Legal Questions Surrounding Referendums on Irish Unity', available at https://brexitlawni.org/library/resources/the-future-of-our-shared-island/ (accessed 02/08/2020).

Berezin, Mabel, 2003. 'Territory, Emotion and Identity', pp. 1–30 in Mabel Berezin and Martin Schain (eds.), *Europe Without Borders: Remapping Territory, Citizenship and Identity in a Transnational Age*. Baltimore: John Hopkins University.

Bew, Paul, 1999. 'The Political History of Northern Ireland Since Partition: The Prospects for North-South Cooperation', pp. 401–408 in A. F. Heath, R. Breen and C. T. Whelan (eds.), *Ireland North and South*. Oxford: Oxford University Press.

Blok, Anton, 2001. *Honour and Violence*. Cambridge: Polity.

Bogdanor, Vernon, 2020. *Britain and Europe in a Troubled World*. New Haven, CT: Yale University Press.

Borneman, John and Nick Fowler, 1997. 'Europeanization', pp. 487–514 in *The Annual Review of Anthropology*, vol. 26.

Bowman, Timothy, 2007. *Carson's Army: The Ulster Volunteer Force, 1910–1922*. Manchester: Manchester University Press.

Brambilla, Chiara, 2015. 'Navigating the Euro/African Border and Migration Nexus Through the Borderscapes Lens: Insights from the *Lampedusa in Festival*', pp. 111–122 in Chiara Brambilla, Jussi Laine, James W. Scott and Gianluca Bocchi (eds.), *Borderscaping: Imaginations and Practices of Border Making*. Farnham: Ashgate.

Brewer, John, 2018. 'The Northern Irish Peace Process', pp. 166–173 in *The Journal of Conflict and Integration*, vol. 2, no. 1.

Britton, Karl, 2000. *Communication: A Physical Study of Language*. Abingdon: Routledge.

Broeders, Dennis, 2011. 'A European "Border" Surveillance System Under Construction', pp. 40–67 in Huub Dijstelbloem and Albert Meijer (eds.), *Migration and New Technological Borders of Europe*. Basingstoke: Palsgrave Macmillan.

Brown, David, 1999. 'Are There Good and Bad Nationalisms?' pp. 281–302 in *Nations and Nationalism*, vol. 5, no. 2.

Bruce, Steve, 1995. 'Paramilitaries, Peace, and Politics: Ulster Loyalists and the 1994 Truce', pp. 187–202 in *Studies in Conflict & Terrorism*, vol. 18, no. 3.

Brunet-Jailly, Emmanuel, 2005. 'Theorizing Borders: An Interdisciplinary Perspective', pp. 640–641 in *Geopolitics*, vol. 10, no. 4.

Buchanan, Sandra, 2014. *Transforming Conflict through Social and Economic Development: Practice and Policy Lessons from Northern Ireland and the Border Counties*. Manchester: Manchester University Press.

Buckland, Patrick, 2001. 'A Protestant State: Unionists in Government, 1921–39', pp. 211–226 in D. G. Boyce and A. O'Day (eds.), *Defenders of the Union: A Survey of British and Irish Unionism Since 1801*. Abingdon: Routledge.

Burke, Mary, 2007. *Pride of Our Place 2002–2006*. Armagh: Centre for Cross Border Studies.

Buzan, Barry, 1993. 'State Security and Internationalization', pp. 41–58 in Ole Waever, Barry Buzan, Morten Kelstrup and Pierre Lemaitre (eds.), *Identity, Migration and the New Security Agenda in Europe*. London: Pinter.

Cantwell Smith, Brian, 2019. *The Promise of Artificial Intelligence: Reckoning and Judgement*. Cambridge, MA: MIT.

Caporaso, James A., 1996. 'The European Union and Forms of State: Westphalian, Regulatory and Post-Modern', pp. 29–52 in *The Journal of Common Market Studies*, vol. 34, no. 1.

Carl, Noah, 2018. *CSI Brexit 4: Reasons Why People Voted Leave or Remain*. Centre for Social Investigation, available at http://csi.nuff.ox.ac.uk/wp-content/uploads/2018/04/Carl_Reasons_Voting.pdf (accessed 20/08/2019).

Cash, John D., 1996. *Identity, Ideology and Conflict: The Structuration of Politics in Northern Ireland*. Cambridge: Cambridge University Press.

Castan Pinos, Jaume and Cathal McCall, 2021. 'The Division of Ireland and its Foes: The Centenary of Resistance to Partition', in *Nations and Nationalism*, available at https://doi.org/10.1111/nana.12687

Coakley, John, 2009. '"Irish Republic", "Eire" or "Ireland"? The Contested Name of John Bull's Other Island', pp. 49–58 in *The Political Quarterly*, vol. 80, no. 1.

Coakley, John, Brian Ó Caoindealbháin and Robin Wilson, 2006. *The Operation of the North-South Implementation Bodies*. Institute for British-Irish Studies IBIS Working Paper No. 56. Dublin: Institute for British-Irish Studies.

Coakley, John and Jennifer Todd, 2020. *Negotiating a Settlement in Northern Ireland, 1969–2019*. Oxford: Oxford University Press.

Coman, R., T. Kostera and L. Tomini, 2014. *Europeanization and European Integration: From Incremental to Structural Change*. London: Palgrave Macmillan.

Connelly, Tony, 2017. 'Ireland, Britain and the Perils of the Brexit Fairy', available at https://www.rte.ie/news/analysis-and-comment/2017/0207/850683-tony-connelly-brexit/ (accessed 07/02/2019).

Connelly, Tony, 2020a. 'Brexit: A Tangle of High Wire Deadlines and Ultimatums', available at www.rte.ie/news/2020/0925/1167545-tony-connelly-brexit/.

Connelly, Tony, 2020b. 'Brexit Talks: Glimmer of Light, or False Dawn', available at www.rte.ie/news/analysis-and-comment/2020/1010/1170611-tony-connelly-brexit-analysis/.

Côté-Boucher, Karine, 2016. 'The Paradox of Discretion: Customs and the Changing Occupational Identity of Canadian Border Officers', pp. 49–67 in *The British Journal of Criminology*, vol. 56, no. 1.

Côté-Boucher, Karine, 2020. *Border Frictions: Gender, Generation and Technology on the Frontline*. London: Routledge.

Dahl, Roald, 2016. *George's Marvellous Medicine*. London: Puffin.

Delanty, Gerald and Chris Rumford, 2005. *Re-thinking Europe: Social Theory and the Implications of Europeanization*. Abingdon: Routledge.

Dell'Olio, Fiorella, 2005. *The Europeanization of Citizenship: Between the Ideology of Nationality, Immigration and European Identity*. Abingdon: Routledge.

Department for Exiting the European Union, 2018. 'Technical Explanatory Note: North-South Cooperation Mapping Exercise', available at https://www.gov.uk/government/publications/technical-explanatory-note-north-south-cooperation-mapping-exercise

Department for Exiting the European Union and Northern Ireland Office, 2017. 'Northern Ireland and Ireland – position paper', available at https://www.gov.uk/government/publications/northern-ireland-and-ireland-a-position-paper

Doyle, John and Eileen Connolly, 2019. 'The Effects of Brexit on the Good Friday Agreement and the Northern Ireland Peace Process', in Cornelia-Adriana Baciu and John Doyle (eds.), *Peace, Security and Defence Cooperation in Post-Brexit Europe Risks and Opportunities*. New York: Springer.

Doyle, Oran, 2020. 'Irish Unification: Processes and Considerations', available at https://constitution-unit.com/2020/05/16/irish-unification-processes-and-considerations/ (accessed 10/08/2020).

Erőss, Ágnes, Béla Filep, Károly Kocsis and Patrik Ta'trai, 2011. 'On Linkages and Barriers: The Dynamics of Neighbourhood Along the State Borders of Hungary Since EU Enlargement', pp. 69–93 in Heidi Armbruster and Ulrike Hanna Meinhoff (eds.), *Negotiating Multicultural Europe: Borders, Networks, Neighbourhoods*. Basingstoke: Palgrave Macmillan.

European Commission, 2017. 'Joint Report from the Negotiators of the European Union and the United Kingdom Government on Progress During Phase 1 of Negotiations Under Article 50 TEU on the United Kingdom's Orderly Withdrawal from the European Union', 8 December 2017, TF50 (2017) 19 – Commission to EU 27, available at https://ec.europa.eu/commission/publications/joint-report-negotiators-european-union-and-united-kingdom-government-progress-during-phase-1-negotiations-under-article-50-teu-united-kingdoms-orderly-withdrawal-european-union_en (accessed 08/12/2019).

European Commission, 2018. 'Draft Agreement on the withdrawal of the United Kingdom of Great Britain and Northern Ireland from the European Union and the European Atomic Energy Community, as agreed at negotiators' level on 14 November 2018', available at https://ec.europa.eu/info/sites/info/files/draft_withdrawal_agreement_0.pdf

European Commission, 2019. 'Negotiations on Ireland/Northern Ireland, Mapping of North-South cooperation, TF50 (2019) 63 – Commission to EU 27', available at https://ec.europa.eu/commission/sites/beta-political/files/mapping_of_north-south_cooperation_0.pdf (accessed 17/09/2019).

European Parliament, 2017. 'Outcome of the Special European Council (Article 50) Meeting of 29 April 2017', available at www.europarl.europa.eu/RegData/etudes/ATAG/2017/603226/EPRS_ATA(2017)603226_EN.pdf (accessed 21/08/2020).

Fanning, Ronan, 2016. *Éamon de Valera: A Will to Power*. Cambridge, MA: Harvard University Press.

Farrell, Michael, 1983. *Arming the Protestants: The Formation of the Ulster Special Constabulary and the Royal Ulster Constabulary 1920–27*. London: Pluto.

Farrell, Michael, 2018. 'Reflections on the Northern Ireland Civil Rights Movement Fifty Years On', available at www.qub.ac.uk/Research/GRI/mitchell-institute/FileStore/Filetoupload,864825,en.pdf (accessed 40/04/2020).

Featherstone, Kevin and Claudio M. Radaelli, 2003. *The Politics of Europeanization*. Oxford: Oxford University Press.

Ferriter, Diarmaid, 2019. *The Border: The Legacy of a Century of Anglo-Irish Politics*. London: Profile Books.

Gallagher, Frank, 1957. *The Indivisible Island: The History of the Partition of Ireland*. London: Gollancz.

Goodhall, David, 1993. 'The Irish question', in *The Ampleforth Journal*, vol. XCVIII, no. 1.

Gormley-Heenan, Cathy and Arthur Aughey, 2017. 'Northern Ireland and Brexit: Three Effects on 'the Border in the Mind', pp. 497–511 in *The British Journal of Politics and International Relations*, vol. 19, no. 3.

Gorzelak, Grzegorz, 2006. 'Normalizing Polish-German Relations: Cross-Border Co-operation in Regional Development', pp. 195–206 in James Wesley Scott (ed.), *EU Enlargement, Region Building and Shifting Borders of Inclusion and Exclusion*. Aldershot: Ashgate.
Guelke, Adrian, 1988. *Northern Ireland: The International Perspective*. Dublin: Gill & Macmillan.
Guelke, Adrian, 2012. 'The USA and the Northern Ireland Peace Process', pp. 424–438 in *Ethnopolitics*, vol. 11, no. 4.
Hadfield, Brigid, 1992. 'The Northern Ireland Constitution', pp. 1–12 in Brigid Hadfield (ed.), *Northern Ireland: Politics and the Constitution*. Buckingham: Open University Press.
Hadfield, Brigid, 2001. 'Seeing it Through? The Multifaceted Implementation of the Belfast Agreement', pp. 84–106 in Rick Wilford (ed.), *Aspects of the Belfast Agreement*. Oxford: Oxford University Press.
Häkli, Jouni, 2015. 'The Border in the Pocket: The Passport as a Boundary Object', pp. 85–99 in Anne-Laure Amilhat Szary and Frédéric Giraut (eds.), *Borderities and the Politics of Contemporary Mobile Borders*. Basingstoke: Palgrave Macmillan.
Hamber, Brandon, 2009. *Transforming Societies after Political Violence: Truth, Reconciliation, and Mental Health*. New York: Springer.
Hann, Chris, 1998. 'Nationalism and Civil Society in Central Europe: From Ruritania to the Carpathian Euroregion', pp. 243–257 in John A. Hall (ed.), *The State of the Nation: Ernest Gellner and the Theory of Nationalism*. Cambridge: Cambridge University Press.
Harmsen, Robert and Thomas M. Wilson (eds.), 2000. *Europeanization: Institution, Identities and Citizenship*. Amsterdam: Rodopi.
Harris, E., 1995. 'Why Unionists Are Not Understood', pp. 27–47 in Arthur Aughey et al. (eds.), *Selling Unionism*. Belfast: Ulster Young Unionist Council.
Havlik, Vlastimil, Vit Hloušek and Petr Kaniok (eds.), 2017. *Europeanised Defiance: Czech Euroscepticism since 2004*. Opladen: Verlag Barbara Budrich.
Hayward, Katy, 2018. *Brexit at the Border: Voices of Local Communities in the Central Border Region of Ireland/Northern Ireland*. Belfast: Centre for International Borders Research, Queen's University Belfast.
Hayward, Katy, 2019a. 'The True Cause of our Backstop Obsession', 8 March, available at www.prospectmagazine.co.uk/politics/the-true-cause-of-our-backstop-obsession (accessed 17/07/2019).
Hayward, Katy, 2019b. 'The Revised Protocol on Ireland/Northern Ireland', available at http://qpol.qub.ac.uk/the-revised-protocol-on-ireland-northern-ireland/ (accessed 01/07/2020).
Hayward, Katy, 2020a. 'Brexit Has Placed Northern Ireland At The UK-EU Interface', available at https://ukandeu.ac.uk/brexit-has-placed-northern-ireland-at-the-uk-eu-interface/ (accessed 02/07/2020).
Hayward, Katy, 2020b. 'What Happened when the UK Internal Market Bill met the Northern Ireland/Ireland Protocol', available at https://ukandeu.ac.uk/what-happened-when-the-uk-internal-market-bill-met-the-ni-irl-protocol/ (accessed 20/09/2020).

Hennessey, Thomas, 1997. *A History of Northern Ireland, 1920–1996*. Dublin: Gill & Macmillan.

Heslinga, Marcus Willem, 1962. *The Irish Border as a Cultural Divide: A Contribution to the Study of Regionalism in the British Isles*. Assen: Van Gorcum.

HMG Government, 2019. 'Operation Yellowhammer: HMG Reasonable Worst Case Planning Assumptions', 2 August 2019, available at https://assets.publishing.service.gov.uk/government/uploads/system/uploads/attachment_data/file/831199/20190802_Latest_Yellowhammer_Planning_assumptions_CDL.pdf (accessed 17/09/2019).

Houses of the Oireachtas, 2017. 'Brexit and the Future of Ireland: Uniting Ireland & Its People in Peace & Prosperity' (32/JCIGFA/02), available at https://webarchive.oireachtas.ie/parliament/media/committees/implementationofthegoodfridayagreement/jcigfa2016/brexit-and-the-future-of-ireland.pdf (accessed 01/08/2020).

Hutchinson, John, 2005. *Nations as Zones of Conflict*. London: Sage.

Jackson, Alvin, 2001. 'Irish Unionism, 1879–1922', pp. 115–136 in D. G. Boyce and A. O'Day (eds.), *Defenders of the Union: A Survey of British and Irish Unionism Since 1801*. Abingdon: Routledge.

Janschitz, S. and A. Kofler, 2004. 'Protecting Diversities and Nurturing Commonalities in a Multicultural Living Space', in V. Pavlakovich-Kochi, B. J. Morehouse and D. Wastl-Walter (eds.), *Challenged Borderlands: Transcending Political and Cultural Boundaries*. Aldershot: Ashgate.

John Whyte Oral Archive, 2007. *John Whyte Oral Archive of British-Irish and Northern Irish Negotiations, 1972–2006*. Dublin: University College Dublin.

Jordan, Glen and Chris Weedon, 1995. *Cultural Politics: Class, Gender, Race and the Postmodern World*. Oxford: Blackwell.

Kassabova, Kapka, 2017. *Border: A Journey Through the Edge of Europe*. London: Granta Books.

Kearney, Richard, 1996. *Postnationalist Ireland: Politics, Culture, Philosophy*. Abingdon: Routledge.

Keating, Michael, 2010. *The Government of Scotland: Public Policy Making after Devolution*. Edinburgh: Edinburgh University Press.

Keating, Michael, 2016. 'Where Next for a Divided United Kingdom?' in *The Irish Times*, 2 July.

Kelly, Fiach, 2019. 'Britain has Always Struggled to Take Ireland Seriously, Say Irish ex-Diplomats', in *The Irish Times*, available at www.irishtimes.com/news/politics/britain-has-always-struggled-to-take-ireland-seriously-say-irish-ex-diplomats-1.3981993 (accessed 12/08/2019).

Kelly, Stephen, 2013. *Fianna Fáil, Partition and Northern Ireland (1926–1971)*. Sallins: Irish Academic Press.

Kennedy, Dennis, 1999. 'Politics of North-South Relations in post-Partition Ireland', pp. 71–96 in P. J. Roche and B. Barton (eds.), *The Northern Ireland Question: Nationalism, Unionism and Partition*. Aldershot: Ashgate.

Kennedy, Dennis, 2014. 'Is it Time to Revisit the Idea of a Federal Ireland?' in *The Irish Times*, 13 November, available at www.irishtimes.com/news/politics/is-it-time-to-revisit-the-idea-of-a-federal-ireland-1.1998276 (accessed 20/08/2020).

Kennedy, Michael, 2000. *Division and Consensus: The Politics of Cross-Border Relations in Ireland, 1925–1969*. Dublin: Institute of Public Administration.

Kennedy-Pipe, Caroline, 2013. *The Origins of the Present Troubles in Northern Ireland*. Abingdon: Routledge.

Keogh, Dermot, 2005. *Twentieth Century Ireland: Revolution and State Building*. Dublin: Gill & Macmillan.

Kilcourse, James, 2013. 'Ireland Raises its Voice in the UK's EU Debate', in *IIEA Blog*, 6 November 2013, available at www.iiea.com/blogosphere/ireland-raises-its-voice-in-the-uks-eu-debate (accessed 29/04/2019).

Klatt, Martin and Hayo Herrmann, 2011. 'Half Empty or Half Full? Over 30 Years of Regional Cross-Border Cooperation Within the EU: Experiences at the Dutch – German and Danish – German Border', pp. 65–87 in *The Journal of Borderlands Studies*, vol. 26, no. 1.

Knill, Christoph, 2001. *The Europeanisation of National Administrations: Patterns of Institutional Change and Persistence*. Cambridge: Cambridge University Press.

Kolossov, Vladimir, 2005. 'Border Studies: Changing Perspectives and Theoretical Approaches', pp. 606–632 in *Geopolitics*, vol. 10, no. 4.

Laffan, Brigid, Rory O'Donnell and Michael Smith, 2000. *Europe's Experimental Union: Rethinking Integration*. Abingdon: Routledge.

Laffan, Brigid and Diane Payne, 2001. *Creating Living Institutions: EU Cross-Border Cooperation after the Good Friday Agreement*. Armagh: Centre for Cross-Border Studies.

Laffan, Michael, 1983. *The Partition of Ireland, 1911–1925*. Dundalk: Dundalgan Press.

Lagana, Giada, 2021. *The European Union and the Northern Ireland Peace Process*. Basingstoke: Palgrave Macmillan.

Leary, Peter, 2016. *Unapproved Routes: Histories of the Irish Border 1922–1972*. Oxford: Oxford University Press.

Lederach, John Paul, 1995. *Preparing for Peace: Conflict Transformation Across Cultures*. Syracuse: Syracuse University Press.

Liddle, Roger, 2015. *The Risk of Brexit: Britain and Europe in 2015*. London: Rowan and Littlefield.

MacMillan, Margaret, 2020. *War: How Conflict Shaped Us*. London: Penguin Random House.

MacShane, Denis, 2019. *Brexiternity: The Uncertain Fate of Britain*. London: I.B Tauris.

Malešević, Siniša, 2010. *The Sociology of War and Violence*. Cambridge: Cambridge University Press.

Mallon, Seamus and Andy Pollak, 2019. *A Shared Home Place*. Dubin: Lilliput Press.

McCall, Cathal, 1998. 'Postmodern Europe and Communal Identities in Northern Ireland', pp. 389–411 in *The European Journal of Political Research*, vol. 33, no. 3.

McCall, Cathal, 2001. 'The Production of Space and the Realignment of Identity in Northern Ireland', pp. 1–24 in *Regional and Federal Studies*, vol. 11.

McCall, Cathal, 2003. 'European Union Cross-Border Cooperation and Conflict Amelioration', pp. 197–216 in *Space and Polity*, vol. 17, no. 2.

McCall, Cathal, 2005. 'From Long War to War of the Lilies: "Post-Conflict" Territorial Compromise and the Return of Cultural Politics', pp. 302–317 in Michael Cox, Adrian Guelke and Fiona Stephen (eds.), *A Farewell to Arms? From 'Long War' to Long Peace in Northern Ireland*, 2nd ed. Manchester: Manchester University Press.

McCall, Cathal, 2011. 'Culture and the Irish Border: Spaces for Conflict Transformation', pp. 201–221 in *Cooperation and Conflict*, vol. 46, no. 2.

McCall, Cathal, 2012. 'Government Must Go Beyond Rhetoric in Supporting Cross-Border Co-Operation', in *The Irish Times*, 17 February.

McCall, Cathal, 2014. *The European Union and Peacebuilding: The Cross-Border Dimension*. Basingstoke: Palgrave Macmillan.

McCall, Cathal, 2018. 'Brexit, Bordering and Bodies on the Island of Ireland', pp. 292–305 in *Ethnopolitics*, vol. 17, no. 3.

McCall, Cathal and Liam O'Dowd, 2008. 'Hanging Flower Baskets, Blowing in the Wind? Third Sector Groups, Cross-Border Partnerships and the EU Peace Programmes in Ireland', pp. 29–54 in *Nationalism and Ethnic Politics*, vol. 13.

McCall, Cathal and Arthur Williamson, 2001. 'Governance and Democracy in Northern Ireland: The Role of the Voluntary and Community Sector after the Agreement', pp. 363–383 in *Governance*, vol. 14, no. 3.

McCann, David Patrick and Cillian McGrattan, 2017. *Sunningdale, the Ulster Workers' Council Strike and the Struggle for Democracy in Northern Ireland*. Manchester: Manchester University Press.

McDonald, M. L., 2020. 'Sinn Féin to Enter New Executive', available at www.sinnfein.ie/contents/55709 (accessed 11/01/2020).

McGarry, John and Brendan O'Leary, 2019. 'Matters of Consent: The Withdrawal Agreement Does Not Violate the Good Friday Agreement', available at https://blogs.lse.ac.uk/politicsandpolicy/brexit-good-friday-agreement/ (accessed 12/07/2020).

McIntosh, Gillian, 1999. *The Force of Culture: Unionist Identities in Contemporary Ireland*. Cork: Cork University Press.

McKenna, Joseph, 2016. *The IRA Bombing Campaign Against Britain, 1939–1940*. Jefferson: McFarland & Company Inc.

McLoughlin, P. J., 2012. *John Hume and the Revision of Irish Nationalism*. Manchester: Manchester University Press.

McLoughlin, P. J., 2016. 'British-Irish Relations and the Northern Ireland Peace Process: The Importance of Intergovernmentalism', pp. 75–90 in Katy Hayward, Elizabeth Meehan and Niall Ó Dochartaigh (eds.), *Divided Ireland: State, Nation and Politics Across the Island*. Abingdon: Routledge.

McNamee, Eoin, 2019. 'We Cannot Go Back to a Hard Border Any More Than Berlin Could Return to the Wall', in *The Irish Times*, 1 April, available at www.irishtimes.com/opinion/we-cannot-go-back-to-a-hard-border-any-more-than-berlin-could-return-to-the-wall-1.3843094 (accessed 02/04/2019).

Meehan, Elizabeth, 2000. *Free Movement Between Ireland and the UK: From the "Common Travel Area" to The Common Travel Area*. Dublin: The Policy Institute.

Milligan, Spike, 1973. *Puckoon*. London: Penguin.

Mulholland, Marc, 2000. *Northern Ireland at the Crossroads: Ulster Unionism in the O'Neill Years, 1960–9*. Basingstoke: Palgrave Macmillan.

Mulroe, Patrick, 2017. *Bombs, Bullets, and the Border: Policing Ireland's Frontier: Irish Security Policy, 1969–1978*. Dublin: Irish Academic Press.

Murphy, Mary C., 2016. *Northern Ireland and the European Union: The Dynamics of a Changing Relationship*. Manchester: Manchester University Press.

Murphy, Mary C., 2018. *Europe and Northern Ireland's Future: Negotiating Brexit's Unique Case*. New York: Agenda Publishing and Columbia University Press.

Murphy, Paul, 2019. *Paul Murphy: Peacemaker*. Cardiff: University of Wales Press.

Nagle, John, 2018. 'Between Conflict and Peace: An Analysis of the Complex Consequences of the Good Friday Agreement', pp. 395–416 in *Parliamentary Affairs*, vol. 71, no. 2.

Nash, Catherine, Bryonie Reid and Brian Graham, 2013. *Partitioned Lives: The Irish Borderlands*. Farnham: Ashgate.

Newman, David, 2006a. 'The Lines that Continue to Separate Us: Borders in our "Borderless" World', pp. 143–161 in *Progress in Human Geography*, vol. 30.

Newman, David, 2006b. 'Borders and Bordering – Towards an Interdisciplinary Dialogue', pp. 171–186 in *The European Journal of Social Theory*, vol. 9.

Nic Dháibhéid, Caoimhe and Colin Reid, 2010. 'The Constitutional and Revolutionary Histories of Modern Ireland', in Caoimhe Nic Dháibhéid and Colin Reid (eds.), *From Parnell to Paisley: Constitution- al and Revolutionary Politics in Modern Ireland*. Dublin: Irish Academic Press.

Nougayrède, Natalie, 2016. 'A New Faultline has Opened up between Germany and Poland', in *The Guardian*, 16 January, available at www.theguardian.com/commentisfree/2016/jan/16/germany-poland-eu-polish-government-european-stability (accessed 10/01/2020).

O'Brien, Conor Cruise, 1972. *States of Ireland*. London: Faber and Faber.

O'Brien, Conor Cruise, 1980. *Neighbours*. London: Faber and Faber.

O'Callaghan, Margaret, 1999. 'Old Parchment and Water: The Boundary Commission of 1925 and the Copperfastening of the Irish Border', pp. 27–55 in *Bullan: An Irish Studies Journal*, vol. 4, no. 2.

O'Callaghan, Margaret, 2018. 'Conor Cruise O'Brien and the Northern Ireland conflict: Formulating a Revisionist Position', pp. 221–231 in *Irish Political Studies*, vol. 33, no. 2.

O'Ceallaigh, Dáithi and Paul Gillespie (eds.), 2015. *Britain and Europe: The Endgame*. Dublin: The Institute of International and European Affairs.

O'Ceallaigh, Dáithi and James Kilcourse, 2013. *Untying the Knot: Ireland, the UK and the EU*. Dublin: The Institute of International and European Affairs.

O'Dowd, Liam, 2010. 'From a "Borderless World" to a "World of Borders": Bringing History Back In', pp. 1031–1050 in *Environment and Planning D: Society and Space*, vol. 28.

O'Dowd, Liam, James Anderson and Thomas M. Wilson (eds.), 2003. *New Borders for a Changing Europe: Cross-Border Cooperation and Governance*. London: Routledge.

O'Dowd, Liam and Cathal McCall, 2008. 'Escaping the Cage of Ethno-national Conflict in Northern Ireland? The Importance of Transnational Networks', pp. 81–99 in *Ethnopolitics*, vol. 7.
O'Halloran Clare, 1987. *Partition and the Limits of Irish Nationalism: An Ideology Under Stress*. Dublin: Gill & Macmillan.
O'Hearn, Denis, 1983. 'Catholic Grievances, Catholic Nationalism: A Comment', pp. 438–445 in *The British Journal of Sociology*, vol. 34, no. 3.
O'Leary, Brendan, 2001. 'The Character of the 1998 Agreement: Results and Prospects', pp. 47–83 in R. Wilford (ed.), *Aspects of the Belfast Agreement*. Oxford: Oxford University Press.
O'Leary, Brendan, 2019a. *A Treatise on Northern Ireland, Volume 1 | Colonialism*. Oxford: Oxford University Press.
O'Leary, Brendan, 2019b. *A Treatise on Northern Ireland, Volume 2 | Control*. Oxford: Oxford University Press.
Parker, Noel, Nick Vaughan-Williams et al., 2009. 'Lines in the Sand? Towards an Agenda for Critical Border Studies', pp. 582–587 in *Geopolitics*, vol. 14, no. 3.
Patterson, Henry, 2013. *Ireland's Violent Frontier: The Border and Anglo-Irish Relations During the Troubles*. Basingstoke: Palgrave Macmillan.
Peoples, Columba and Nick Vaughan Williams, 2015. *Critical Security Studies: An Introduction*. Abingdon: Routledge.
Phinnemore, David, 2020. 'Post-Brexit Trade Deal: The Gaps Worth Noting', in *The Conversation*, 29 December, available at https://theconversation.com/post-brexit-trade-deal-the-gaps-worth-noting-152568 (accessed 03/01/2021).
Phinnemore, David and Lee McGowan, 2013. *A Dictionary of the European Union*. Abingdon: Routledge.
Poggi, Gianfranco, 1990. *The State: Its Nature, Development and Prospects*. Oxford: Polity.
Pollak, Andy, 2001. 'The Policy Agenda for Cross-Border Cooperation: A View from the Centre for Cross-Border Studies', pp. 15–22 in *Administration*, vol. 49, no. 2.
Pollak, Andy, 2011. 'Cross-Border Cooperation as Part of the Irish Peace Process: Opportunities, Impacts and Challenges', pp. 135–144 in *Uprava*, vol. IX, no. 2.
Pollak, Sorcha, 2016. 'Search After Young Man's Death Bonds Border Communities', in *The Irish Times*, 11 January.
Prince, Simon, 2007. *Northern Ireland's '68: Civil Rights, Global Revolt and the Origins of the Troubles*. Dublin: Irish Academic Press.
Purdie, Bob, 1986. 'The Irish Anti-Partition League, South Armagh and the Abstentionist Tactic 1945–58', pp. 67–77 in *Irish Political Studies*, vol. 1, no. 1.
Rajaram, Prem Kumar and Carl Grundy-Warr, 2008. 'Introduction', pp. ix–xl in Prem Kumar Rajaram and Carl Grundy-Warr (eds.), *Borderscapes: Hidden Geographies and Politics at Territory's Edge*. Minneapolis: Minneapolis University Press.
Ramsbotham, Oliver, Tom Woodhouse and Hugh Miall, 2011. *Contemporary Conflict Resolution: The Prevention, Management and Transformation of Deadly Conflicts*, 3rd ed. Cambridge: Polity.
Rankin, K. J., 2005. *The Creation and Consolidation of the Irish Border* (IBIS Working Paper no. 48). Dublin: Institute for British-Irish Studies.

Rawnsley, Andrew, 2020. 'The Escalating Delinquency of Boris Johnson and his Gang of Blue Anarchists', in *The Observer*, 13 September, available at www.theguardian.com/commentisfree/2020/sep/13/the-escalating-delinquency-of-boris-johnson-and-his-gang-of-blue-anarchists (accessed 20/09/2020).

Reid, Colin, 2010. 'The Irish Party and the Volunteers: Politics and the Home Rule Army, 1913–1916', in Caoimhe Nic Dháibhéid and Colin Reid (eds.), *From Parnell to Paisley: Constitutional and Revolutionary Politics in Modern Ireland*. Dublin: Irish Academic Press.

Reimann, Cordula, 2004. 'Assessing the State-of-the-Art in Conflict Transformation', available at www.berghof-handbook.net (accessed 13/02/2020).

Richardson, Jeremy (ed.), 2006. *European Union: Power and Policy-Making*. Abingdon: Routledge.

Rose, Richard, 1983. *Is the United Kingdom a State?* Glasgow: University of Strathclyde.

Ruane Joseph and Jennifer Todd, 2001. 'The Politics of Transition? Explaining Political Crises in the Implementation of the Belfast Good Friday Agreement', pp. 923–940 in *Political Studies*, vol. 49.

Rumford, Chris, 2006. 'Theorizing Borders', pp. 155–169 in *The European Journal of Social Theory*, vol. 9.

Sack, Robert D., 1986. *Human Territoriality: Its Theory and History*. Cambridge: Cambridge University Press.

Salmon, Christian, 2007. *Storytelling, La Machine à Fabriquer des Histoires et à Formatter les Esprits*. Paris: Éditions La Découverte Expulsions.

Sassen, Saskia, 2014. *Brutality and Complexity in the Global Economy*. Cambridge, MA: Harvard University Press.

Schubotz, Dirk, 2014. 'Conclusion', pp. 138–149 in Dirk Schubotz and Paula Devine (eds.), *Not so Different: Teenage Attitudes Across a Decade of Change in Northern Ireland*. Dorset: Russell House.

Scott, James Wesley, 2011. 'Borders, Border Studies and EU Enlargement', in Doris Wastl-Walter (ed.), *The Ashgate Research Companion to Border Studies*. Farnham and Burlington: Ashgate.

Shore, Cris, 2000. *Building Europe: The Cultural Politics of European integration*. Abingdon: Routledge.

Singham, Shanker, Austen Morgan, Victoria Hewson and Alice Brooks, 2017. *How the UK and EU Can Resolve the Irish border Issue After Brexit*. London: Legatum Institute, p. 28, available at www.li.com/activities/publications/mutual-interest-how-the-uk-and-eu-can-resolve-the-irish-border-issue-after-brexit (accessed 08/12/2017).

Sinn Féin, 2016. 'The Case for the North to Achieve Special Designated Status', available at www.sinnfein.ie/files/2016/The_Case_For_The_North_To_Achieve_Special_Designated_Status_Within_The_EU.pdf (accessed 28/01/2020).

Snyder, Francis, 2000. *The Europeanisation of law: The legal effects of European Integration*. European law. Oxford: Hart Publishing.

Sørensen, Georg, 1999. 'Sovereignty: Change and Continuity in a Fundamental Institution', pp. 590–604 in *Political Studies*, vol. 47.

Spencer, Philip and Howard Wollman, 1998. 'Good and Bad Nationalisms: A Critique of Dualism', pp. 255–274 in *The Journal of Political Ideologies*, vol. 3, no. 3.

Spohn, Willfried, and Anna Triandafyllidou (eds.), 2003. *Europeanisation, National Identities and Migration: Changes in Boundary Constructions between Western and Eastern Europe*. Abingdon: Routledge.

Staunton, Denis, 2017. 'UK Rules out Moving Border to Irish Sea', in *The Irish Times*, 29 July.

Stokłosa, Katarzyna, 2014. 'The Border in the Narratives of the Inhabitants of the German-Polish Border region', pp. 257–274 in Katarzyna Stokłosa and Gerhard Besier (eds.), *European Border Regions in Comparison: Overcoming Nationalist Aspects or Re-Nationalization?* Abingdon: Routledge.

Szabó, Gyula and Gábor Koncz, 2006. 'Transboundary Interaction in the Hungarian-Romanian Border Region: A Local View', pp. 163–170 in James Wesley Scott (ed.), *EU Enlargement, Region Building and Shifting Borders of Inclusion and Exclusion*. Aldershot: Ashgate.

Tannam, Etain, 1999. *Cross-Border Cooperation in the Republic of Ireland and Northern Ireland*. Basingstoke: Palgrave Macmillan.

Taylor, Charlie, 2017. 'Post-Brexit Tech Border Deemed "Complete Nonsense" by IT Experts', in *The Irish Times*, 16 August, available at www.irishtimes.com/business/technology/post-brexit-tech-border-deemed-complete-nonsense-by-it-experts-1.3188475 (accessed 20/08/2017).

Teague, Paul, 2019. 'Brexit, the Belfast Agreement and Northern Ireland: Imperilling a Fragile Political Bargain', pp. 690–704 in *The Political Quarterly*, vol. 90, no. 4.

Tilly, Charles, 1990. *Coercion, Capital and European States AD 900–1990*. Oxford: Basil Blackwell.

Tonge, Jon, 2020. 'Beyond Unionism versus Nationalism: The Rise of the Alliance Party of Northern Ireland', pp. 461–466 in *The Political Quarterly*, vol. 91, no. 2.

Topak, Özgün E., Ciara Bracken-Roche, Alana Saulnier and David Lyon, 2015. 'From Smart Borders to Perimeter Security: The Expansion of Digital Surveillance at the Canadian Borders', pp. 880–99 in *Geopolitics*, vol. 20, no. 4.

Tournier-Sol, Karine and Chris Gifford (eds.), 2015. *The UK Challenge to Europeanization: The Persistence of British Euroscepticism*. Basingstoke: Palgrave Macmillan.

van Houtum, Henk and Roos Pijpers, 2007. 'The European Union as a Gated Community: The Two-faced Border and Immigration Regime of the EU', pp. 291–309 in *Antipode*, vol. 39, no. 2.

Vaughan-Williams, Nick, 2009. *Border Politics: The Limits of Sovereign Power*. Edinburgh: Edinburgh University Press.

Voltaire, 1991. *Candide*. New York: Dover.

Waever, Ole, 1995. 'Securitization and Desecuritization', pp. 46–86 in Ronnie D. Lipschutz (ed.), *On Security*. New York: Columbia University Press.

Wallace, Helen, 2000. 'Europeanisation and Globalisation: Complementary or Contradictory Trends?' pp. 369–382 in *New Political Economy*, vol 5, no. 3.

Walsh, Dermot, 2011. 'Police Cooperation across the Irish Border: Familiarity Breeding Contempt for Transparency and Accountability', pp. 301–330 in *The Journal of Law and Society*, vol. 38, no. 2.
Walters, William, 2006. 'Border/Control', pp. 187–203 in *The European Journal of Social Theory*, vol. 9, no. 2.
Wellings, Ben, 2018. 'The Brexit Mess Could Lead to a Break-Up of a no Longer United Kingdom', in *The Conversation*, available at http://theconversation.com/the-brexit-mess-could-lead-to-a-break-up-of-a-no-longer-united-kingdom-107093 (accessed 16/07/2019).
Whysall, Alan, 2019. *A Northern Ireland Border Poll*. London: The Constitution Unit, School of Public Policy, University College London.
Whyte, John, 1983. 'The Permeability of the United Kingdom-Irish Border: A Preliminary Reconnaissance', pp. 330–345 in *Administration*, vol. 31, no. 3.
Whyte, John, 1990. *Interpreting Northern Ireland*. Oxford: Clarendon.
Wilson Thomas M., 2019. 'Old and New Nationalisms in the Brexit Borderlands of Northern Ireland', pp. 25–51 in Katherine Donahue and Patricia Heck (eds.), *Cycles of Hatred and Rage*. New York: Palgrave Macmillan.
Wilson, Tim, 2010. 'The Most Terrible Assassination That Has Yet Stained the Name of Belfast: The McMahon Murders in Context', pp. 83–106 in *Irish Historical Studies*, vol. 37, no. 145.
Working Group on Unification Referendums on the Island of Ireland, 2020. *Interim Report*, November. London: The Constitution Unit, University College London, available at www.ucl.ac.uk/constitution-unit/sites/constitution-unit/files/wgurii_interim_report_nov_2020.pdf.

Index

For Product Safety Concerns and Information please contact our EU representative GPSR@taylorandfrancis.com
Taylor & Francis Verlag GmbH, Kaufingerstraße 24, 80331 München, Germany

www.ingramcontent.com/pod-product-compliance
Ingram Content Group UK Ltd.
Pitfield, Milton Keynes, MK11 3LW, UK
UKHW021245190926
475569UK00001BA/15
* 9 7 8 1 1 3 8 5 8 7 0 4 5 *